To Indy and Beyond

The Life of Racing Legend Jack Zink

To Indy and Beyond

The Life of Racing Legend Jack Zink

By Dr. Bob L. Blackburn

ISBN 0-9720244-0-10

Printed in the United States of America
for Cottonwood Publications, Oklahoma City, Oklahoma.

Printed by Baker Group, LLC - 405.503.3207

Design by Skip McKinstry

Dedicated to the Zink Family and the People of Tulsa

Table of Contents

Author's Preface

For more than thirty years I have been collecting, preserving, and sharing the stories of Oklahoma and its people. I have worked with governors, legislators, mayors, business innovators, church leaders, and thousands of men and women who have contributed to the fabric of our society through hard work, perseverance, and a willingness to give back to their community.

In all of those years, I have never known, nor will I ever again know, a man like Jack Zink.

I met Jack in 2001 while I was working on the Oklahoma History Center, a 215,000 square foot museum and research facility we were building next to the State Capitol in Oklahoma City. In the museum, we had an exhibit area devoted to sports in Oklahoma, and I wanted a substantial object, a large historic artifact, to greet visitors as they came around a corner and discovered the area on sports. I decided I wanted a race car.

I did not want any race car. I wanted a race car with an Oklahoma story, a story of innovation, hard work, setbacks, victories, and teamwork. As I asked friends in the sports world about such a car, everyone pointed me in the same direction—Jack Zink of Tulsa, Oklahoma.

First, I did my homework. I discovered that Jack had won many races, not just with cars, but also with off-road dune buggies, motorcycles, and sailboats. Among his many accomplishments were victories at two tracks that touched my own memories of racing: Taft Stadium in Oklahoma City, and the Indianapolis Motor Speedway, home of the world's most prestigious race, the Indianapolis 500. As a historian and museum curator, I was drawn to the unique story. As a baby boomer and child artist who drew thousands of race car pictures in the 1950s and 1960s, I wanted to meet the man who had walked shoulder to shoulder with A.J. Foyt, Parnelli Jones, and Mario Andretti.

I called Jack Zink at his ranch located in the Osage Hills west of Tulsa. He answered the phone, listened patiently to my story, and agreed to meet me at the Faculty Club restaurant in Oklahoma City. I was at the table when he arrived. He wore khaki pants, a well-worn sports coat that did not quite match, and hiking boots. Completing the Jack Zink look was a baseball cap pulled tight over his brow, a blue bandanna around his neck, and a warm greeting followed by a firm handshake. I liked him immediately.

Over the next two hours we shared stories. He asked me about my family, my career, and my plans for the History Center. I asked him about his family, his career, and his plans for telling his own story. Although the ensuing friendship has probably compressed many memories into that first meeting, it seemed like we shared a common path of interests, experiences, and goals. Among the many connections were car racing, outdoor recreation, a passion for hard work and economy, Oklahoma State University, public service, and a deep pride in our state. By the time we left that first meeting, Jack said he would help us with the exhibit. To work out the details, he wanted me to visit him at the Zink Ranch. He said we would go four-wheeling on a tour of the ranch.

At that time, I was crisscrossing the state giving speeches and lining up support for the $61 million investment in the History Center, so I agreed to swing by the ranch on the way to Stillwell where I was scheduled to give a speech. As I drove along the scenic road leading into the ranch, I noticed a big sign that said, "Welcome Dr. Bob Blackburn, Oklahoma Historical Society," placed where only he and I would have seen it that day. I also drove by a long row of shop doors, one of which was curiously open with a dune buggy sitting out front. Jack greeted me at the door of his rustic lodge, which sits on a bluff with a beautiful view overlooking the Arkansas River Valley. He looked at my suit and tie, frowned, and mysteriously said I had "better change into something more durable." Inside, we rummaged through a stack of blue jeans, t-shirts, and running shoes until I found a reasonable fit. Then I discovered why I needed the change of clothes. The four-wheeling tour of the ranch was going to be in the dune buggy he had driven to many championships around the country, and I was going to drive.

He tossed a helmet to me, the kind of helmet you would see in a NASCAR commercial, and told me to slide into the driver's seat through the glass-less window. Then he strapped me in with what seemed like full-body compression straps. He climbed through the other window, strapped himself in, and said, "start it up and let's go." Fortunately, my first car had been a Volkswagen bug and my graduate school set of wheels had been a Volkswagen van, so I knew the shifting patterns, the feel of the clutch, and the sounds of the engine's rpm's as I roared down the road. Within a few hundred feet, he yelled at me to drive into the tree line on the side of the road at a particular spot. "Trust me," he said, "there is a path on the other side of the brush. I haven't been through there lately to knock it down." I did as instructed and found myself driving that competition dune buggy over trails that took us to the far corners of the 33,000-acre ranch. I had a smile for a week. And I was late for my speech in Stillwell.

I guess I passed the test. Over the next year I had many meetings with Jack, some in Oklahoma City and some at the ranch. I came to know his collection, which consisted of more than twenty vehicles, thousands of photographs, and hundreds of artifacts that ranged from trophies and helmets to racing jackets and pit crew paraphernalia. I gathered articles and newspaper clippings about his racing and started a series of interviews. About the time I had enough information to prepare the exhibit, he and his wife, Jan, asked me to come into their living quarters to talk. Jan, who was devoted to Jack, asked if I would be interested in writing a biography about him. By that time I knew the rough outlines of the story, enough to want to learn more, but I also knew my schedule and the mounting demands to finish the History Center and fulfill my varied duties as executive director of the Oklahoma Historical Society. Because all of my writing is done on weekends and vacations, I said I would have to think about it.

Jan, who was a development officer at the University of Tulsa, was persistent. She pushed aside Jack's natural modesty and convinced me he would sit for extended interviews. She would make all collections accessible. And she would help set up interviews with friends and family. By that time, I was fascinated by what I already knew, and my self-survival instincts were overwhelmed by my natural curiosity. I said yes, I would write the biography.

Over the next year, stealing vacation days here and a weekend there, I gathered primary and secondary documents. At the ranch, we went through countless boxes of material, uncovering scrapbooks, letters, loose clippings, and racing keepsakes such as programs, tickets, and magazines. I got lucky at the Tulsa World, where the archivist uncovered at least ten fat folders stuffed with clippings about the elder John Zink, Jack and his business career, Jack and the racing team, and more. I found materials at Cascia Hall and the University of Tulsa. I traveled to Indianapolis where I spent three glorious days sorting through archival materials and photographs tracing the exploits of the Zink Racing Team. As the story came into focus, I started the interviews, first with Jack and then with others such as his sister Jill, his racing buddies such as Dennie Moore, and his peers in the civic and business community such as King Kirchner.

As I worked and organized the material, the story found a natural rhythm, alternating passages that captured Jack's personality with stories about his racing exploits and business experiences. Holding the stories together were common threads such as friendships, action, careful preparation, tenacity, self discipline, competition, and concern for others, all set against the backdrop of Jack's world of Tulsa, the business community, and racing. Although the narrative focuses primarily on Jack, the stage is shared by others who influenced his life, people like his father and mother, his racing pals like Jimmy Reece and Dennie Moore, and the many men and women who shared Jack's love for his city and state.

As I neared the end of the writing phase, Jack's health began to decline. With Jan's help and the assistance of Jack's son, Darton, I finished the draft of the last chapter in late 2004, just in time for Jack to read it. Like he had done with earlier chapter drafts, he pointed out mistakes, suggested further research where needed, and seemed embarrassed that he was at the center of the narrative stage. Most importantly to me, he said that I had captured the contours of his life, the ups and downs, the moments of sheer ecstasy and the darker days of failure and disappointment. A few weeks later, Jack was gone.

—⚬⚬⚬—

This book would not have been possible without the help and encouragement of many people. I want to thank Jan Zink for launching the project and encouraging me and Jack with her kind nature and seemingly endless optimism. Darton Zink, after his father's death, stepped into the partnership and added his editorial comments and assisted with the accumulation of photographs. His associate at Zeeco, Scott Johnson, should consider a second career as an editor. His sharp eye and disciplined focus improved the manuscript and discovered inconsistencies. Additional improvements were made by Scott's son, Eric Johnson, a recent college graduate with great promise. Dennie Moore, Jack's good friend and chief mechanic since 1953, read the manuscript and added significant facts and details. The beauty of the book is the good work of my friend and long-time design collaborator, Skip McKinstry.

At home, my wife Debbie has learned to tolerate the use of weekends and holidays for my work and ignore the scattered files and boxes littering our shared office. She heard much of the book as I read it to her out loud, still the best test of an author's rhetorical tools. Dr. Tim Zwink, a friend and fellow conspirator in the History Center project, edited the manuscript and offered many good suggestions. Of course, I take full responsibility for any omissions or mistakes that might have slipped into the narrative.

As you will see, I end the book with a poem that Jack recited when he was inducted into the Oklahoma Hall of Fame. The last line, in particular, is an appropriate summary of Jack's life: "The man who wins in the man who tries." I hope this book will encourage others to do the same. Jack would want it that way.

Bob Blackburn, November 2008

A Good Start

"You must understand who you are, be a dreamer and have lots of patience."

Jack Zink

CHAPTER ONE

It was an unusually hot fall evening in Tulsa when Swannie told John to rush her to St. John Hospital. The baby she had been carrying for nine months was ready to join the family. The delivery went well, unusually fast, and their second child was born on October 17, 1928. They named him John Smith Zink.

The name was a link to family tradition. The first name honored the father, John Steele Zink, a large, gregarious man with ruddy hair and hands that had grown strong and tough from his younger years growing up on a farm. The middle name honored the mother, Swannie Smith Zink, a small, introspective woman at five-feet three inches tall, who was a bundle of energy packed in a muscular, wiry body. While Jack would favor his mother both physically and temperamentally, his older sister, Jill, born four years before, was more like her father. Six years later the family would grow once again with the birth of a third child, Sally, a quiet, serious girl more like Swannie but close to her father.

The Zink household provided a strong foundation that nurtured initiative and action, in large part due to the combination of strengths and talents brought to the union of John and Swannie. While the father was a rugged individualist, confident in his physical and business skills, Swannie was the creative type, a scholar with a burning curiosity who treasured books, poetry, and the pursuit of knowledge.

John Steele Zink was born in 1893 near Newton, Iowa, one of three children born to John and Eva Zink. Like most of their generation, the Zinks were farmers, but they wanted greater opportunities for their children. In 1906 they moved to a farm near Norman, Oklahoma Territory, so the kids could attend a nearby university. John, who was thirteen at the time of the move, later fulfilled the wish of his parents and attended Oklahoma University, where he completed a degree in chemistry. He quickly found a job with Oklahoma Natural Gas Company, which had been founded in 1906 to gather and distribute natural gas to domestic markets in the growing towns and cities of the soon-to-be-formed state. [1]

In 1917 the company transferred John to Tulsa, a boom town that was still riding a frenzied wave of economic and industrial expansion following the discovery of the Cushing Oil Field only thirty miles to the southwest. While living in the local YMCA, the young, outgoing college graduate used his farm boy practical skills and education to start his climb through the corporate ranks, ultimately landing the post of manager for industrial sales.

One weekend, a friend, James R. Cole, invited John to join him on a trip to visit his in-laws in Baxter Springs, Missouri. James' father-in-law was Charles Smith, at that time the local postmaster, print shop owner, and publisher of the *Baxter Springs News*. Mr. Smith was also a Democrat and Episcopalian, both of which he let everyone know were "set in stone." He was a well-read scholar and a collector of books which he readily shared with friends and family. He and his wife, Estelle, had six children, four girls and two boys, including a daughter with the Southern-sounding name of Swannie. [2]

Details of the early friendship between John and Swannie do not survive, but obviously their introduction led to subsequent visits and ultimately romance. There is some evidence that Mr. Smith was not too enthused about the young man from the old Indian Territory. When John

The prolific production of the Cushing Oil Field after 1912 helped make Tulsa the "Oil Capital of the World." (Courtesy Oklahoma Historical Society)
(Unless marked otherwise, all photographs are from the Zink Family Archives).

Young Jack Zink at the age of four (page 2), going off-road at the family home in Tulsa.

gave Swannie an engagement ring packed in a candy box, he included a receipt showing that it was paid in full. John wanted to show his future father-in-law that he was a man with the means to start a family. John and Swannie were married on Thanksgiving Day, 1921. [3]

The newlyweds were a dynamic pairing in a dynamic city undergoing the early stages of a total transformation. Only twenty years before, Tulsa had been a small trading village in the old Creek Nation, established where the westward expanding Frisco Railroad crossed a natural ford on the Arkansas River. Muskogee, located about forty miles downriver, was the biggest and most promising town in the territory, while Tulsa pioneers such as the Perrymans, Halls, and Archers counted fewer than 1,000 residents in their fledgling community. To those ambitious merchant families, it was of little interest that the town was located near the old Council Oak Tree and ceremonial grounds that dated to the establishment of the Creek Town, Tulasi, in the 1830s. [4]

These quiet frontier origins began to fade in 1902 with the discovery of the modest Red Fork Oil Field and totally disappeared in 1905 with the discovery of the prolific Glenn Pool Field. Overnight, Tulsa became a world-famous crossroads for land men, drillers, roughnecks, rig builders, pipe liners, refiners, and general laborers. With the workers came supply houses, newspapers, and banks, as well as homebuilders, doctors, lawyers, and teachers. They came from all corners of the world, bringing with them a duke's mixture of cultural baggage and a general attitude that judged people not by their family tree or their place in the social register, but by their ability to get things done. For a young, talented couple like John and Swannie Zink, it was an opportunity to dig in, raise a family, and do it their way.

The frontier leveling influence, where nearly everyone was from somewhere else, encouraged the strongly individualistic tendencies of John and Swannie. Many years later, after John had made both a fortune and a reputation with the press, a reporter called him "the original hippie...a restless genius, and the last of the rugged individualists." That non-conformist attitude was reflected in the way he dressed the last twenty-five years of his life—terry cloth shorts he designed himself, pullover shirts, knee-high socks, and high-top basketball shoes with no laces. When it turned cold outside, he simply added long-handle underwear. "Clothing," he told one reporter, "should serve comfort, not fashion." [5]

By the 1920s, when John Steele and Swannie Zink moved to Tulsa, it was the fastest growing city in Oklahoma (Courtesy Oklahoma Historical Society).

For more than fifty years, the International Petroleum Exposition drew the oil industry to Tulsa to see the latest in drilling and production technology (Courtesy Oklahoma Historical Society).

Jack, in the center, grew up with two sisters, many neighborhood friends, and the freedom to roam nearby fields and the Arkansas River valley.

Eliot School, where Jack attended grade school.

Swannie, although more traditional in her personal tastes, never followed the crowd and did not dilute her energies with club meetings or polite social responsibilities. She was a collector, filling the family home with fine furniture and art objects, especially silver and celery holders. She gave lectures on collecting and served on the original board of directors for the Philbrook Museum of Art, established in the former mansion of Waite Phillips in 1938. Among her own collections was a vast library of books and genealogical materials on her family lines. [6]

As if punctuating her streak of individualism, Swannie was a poet. In 1947 she published a slim volume of her poetry, not for the general public, but for her family and friends, the people who knew her best. Some of the poems were whimsical, full of humor, while some were soulful expressions of her deepest emotions. All were good poetry using words and rhythm to express the true self. One, titled "Antebellum," captured her non-conformist spirit:

I am a rebel, I rebel at my mate,
Rebel at love, still, I cannot hate;
Rebel at clothes, rebel at food,
At clubs, conventions, bad and good;
Rebel at work, rebel at hats,
Most of all at two-legged cats;
Rebel at noise from four radios,
And at the cars that spatter my hose;
Rebel at fat, rebel at shrines,
Rebel at warnings and at signs;
I am a rebel, yet I have a date
To keep as rebels must—with Fate. [7]

Swannie's eclectic tastes were evident in her gardens, which eventually swallowed the Zink compound of houses and outbuildings at 31st and Madison. There were shaded nooks with fountains, flowerbeds full of color, hidden pathways seductively leading in all directions, and deep green foliage that seemed cool even on the hottest summer days. When asked by one reporter how she designed the gardens, Swannie said, "I carried a spade full of dirt with its seeds around looking for the right place until I got tired and just dropped it." If anything, the gardens were a reflection of her energy. One of her favorite quotations was from Kipling, "Our

England is a garden, gardens are not made, by saying 'Oh how beautiful,' and sitting in the shade." [8]

Swannie even dabbled with house design. When the newlyweds moved to Tulsa in 1921, they bought a lot on North Yukon Avenue and Swannie served as contractor to build a small house. After Jill was born in 1924, they needed a larger home so they bought recently platted lots on the far south side of town near the corner of 31st and Madison. At the time, the area was still largely rural, with cultivated fields of corn to the south and the Arkansas River to the west. 31st Street dead-ended at Madison before a trail descended into the fertile river valley. [9]

The first house built on the lots was a small two-bedroom bungalow. When Jack was born, they built a second house on the lots but kept the first house in the family. There was still plenty of room on the combined properties for a garage, servants' quarters for a maid and grounds keeper, and a corral for two horses. Over the years the main house, like the gardens, would continue to grow and expand, often in unusual directions, but always with function and family in mind. It was in this household, reflecting the equally strong personalities of John and Swannie, that Jack and his two sisters were raised. [10]

———❧———

As Jack would later remember, his parents reached a remarkable equilibrium raising their children by balancing discipline and caution with freedom and adventure. Unlike urban youth in the 21st century, the kids in Jack's childhood neighborhood had mobility and a wide-ranging playground that encompassed open fields, the river valley, and nearby housing additions filled with potential playmates. In the days before television, video games, and air conditioning, kids spent most of their waking hours either in school or outdoors. The Zink kids were no exception.

Even John, the more cautious of the two parents, encouraged a sense of exploration in his children. In 1934, when Jack was six, his father traded a radio for an old Model T dump truck that was not running and parked it behind the house. Jack and his friends had an instant playground, tearing into the engine, removing the wheels, and dismantling

Jack with Fritz, his German Shepherd police dog and partner in roaming the rural areas surrounding the Zink home.

Until he went to college, Jack lived in the same house at 31st and Madison; now considered "mid-town," at the time it was the "south side" of Tulsa.

the dump bed to use as a cover for an underground fort. Jack would always remember the sad day two years later when he saw a pair of men rolling the old dump truck down the road, the prize of a trade negotiated this time by his mother who wanted the old wreck out of her gardens. [11]

Sharing this world of adventure were the usual animals. At home was Fritz, the giant German Shepherd Police Dog, which was left behind by neighbors who moved. The dog was both a companion and hunter. Many days Fritz returned to the house with his daily catch, maybe a possum, a raccoon, or one time, a goat. Other members of the menagerie included cows, hogs, and the usual range of critters such as the copperhead snake Jack and a friend lost in a neighbor's house. [12]

Jack's childhood world expanded on the back of Smokey, his horse, which was kept behind the house with his mother's horse. A typical destination was the old fairgrounds, located almost three miles to the east, and he even rode the horse when attending Eliot Grade School, tethering him on a stake close to a cornfield while he attended class. Many days were interrupted when the principal announced over the intercom, "Jack, your horse is loose again." [13]

Occasionally, the adventuresome spirits of the Zink children drew cautionary corrections from their parents. One such episode remembered by Jill followed the discovery of an outcrop of red clay. Jill and Jack proceeded to paint each other red, which ended with their mother giving them a whipping. Jack developed another habit of picking up junk as he walked home from school. Some days he walked along the railroad tracks where he found treasures fallen from high speed trains. Even more dangerous were his scouts near the shantytown settlements of homeless people in the river bottom where he found a bountiful crop of booty. When his mother found out about the harvest, she cut six switches from the backyard willow tree and used all of them to make her point about the balance between caution and courage. [14]

Sixty years later, Jack would describe his youthful spirit as "ornery," an attitude he took to school first at Lee Grade School, then Eliot Grade School, followed by Horace Mann Junior High, and finally, Cascia Hall High School. At Cascia, which Jack considered perfect for him, he was a regular member of Father Wynn's Jug Class, made up of boys who needed the disciplined routine of cutting grass, raking leaves, and taking care of the school grounds to remind them there was more to life than adventure. Jack, through a combination of spirited antics and dependability, eventually earned his way to becoming the student supervisor of the after school club.[15]

Cascia, founded in 1925 as a Catholic boys school, provided its students with a high quality education and a sense of belonging. It was small enough that everyone knew each other, but large enough to offer a wide range of life experiences. Socially, there were regular dances, especially the Christmas and Spring balls, which Jack supported as co-chairman of the refreshments committee during his senior year. Jack also served on the Student Council, was business manager of the yearbook, and earned a spot as one of three section leaders in the uniformed Cascia Military Unit, organized in 1942 to prepare the boys for service in the field artillery. The student captain of the unit was Bob LaFortune, future mayor of Tulsa. [16]

Jack's first love at Cascia, however, was football. He went out for the team as a freshman and was one of only two classmates to make the varsity. As a youth, Jack was not very tall, barely over five feet, but he was stocky, quick, and rugged. As quoted in the yearbook, he earned the nickname "Jarrin' John" for his rough style, which was to play hard every down whether he was on offense or defense, in practice or in a game. Against a Fort Smith team, Jack's coaches told him to fire off the line and hit the opposing center on top of the head as soon as the ball was snapped. He did as told, but was warned by the referee not to do it again. Ignoring the warning, Jack again fired out and hit the center as soon as he snapped the ball. This time, the referee flagged him with a fifteen-yard penalty for rough play. On the next two plays the same thing happened, with Jack hitting the center and the referee imposing two more penalties. It turned out the referee was the father of the center suffering the hard play of Jarrin' John. [17]

That same stubborn pride was revealed in class one day when the boys got into an eraser fight. Father Stephen Fogarty heard the commotion, came into the room, and saw a number of boys at the scene of the crime. When he asked who was involved, several boys raised their hands, but when he demanded to know who started it, all hands went down. Jack, unwilling to dodge the responsibility, raised his hand and said, "Father, it was me." Later, at a class assembly, Father Fogarty described the transgression, but singled out Jack for having courage and principles, saying, "Truth will always get you where you want to go and keep you out of

Jack liked school, but he loved football. He made the varsity team as a freshman and earned the nickname "Jarrin' John" for his toughness and hard play.

JOHN SMITH ZINK
"Jarrin' John"

Member of Student Council . . . Football (1, 2, 4) . . . Business manager of the Towers . . . Intramural "Buccaneer."

Jack was a member of the motorcycle daredevils. He has been a constant member of Father Winn's jug class. He often can be seen walking into the canteen and blaring out the immortal words, "All right, youse guys!"

Remember: His short pants, the first day of school in his freshman year.

Page 38

The Cascia Hall yearbook summarized Jack's favorite activities—motorcycles and football.

trouble. It's tough to be tough, but Jack did it." [18]

The 1945 Cascia yearbook offers other glimpses into Jack's rugged ways. In comments about each senior, the editors wrote: "He often can be seen walking into the canteen and blaring out the immortal words, 'All right, youse guys!'" A caricature on the same page depicted Jack as a strutting wise guy pointing a finger and doing an imitation of James Cagney in a gangster movie. That same year the student newspaper ran a cryptic note, "It seems Zink went wild again: result, two stitches over McKeown's left eye." The tough guy image extended to another initiative taken by Jack at Cascia where he was founder and member of the "Motorcycle Daredevils." [19]

Motorcycles became a part of Jack's life in 1943 when Phil Adrian, Jill's best friend who lived across the street from the Zinks, entered the Army Air Corps and left his 45-cubic-inch G.I. Harley Davidson with Jack. The understanding was that if anything happened to Phil, Jack would get the bike. Phil survived his first flirt with death and escaped to Sweden after his plane was shot down over Germany. The next year, while ferrying bombers to Europe, his plane went down somewhere at sea. Tragically, he was never heard from again. [20]

The motorcycle, like the memory of Phil Adrian, became an integral part of Jack's life. It gave him mobility. It gave him freedom. Most of all, it opened up new possibilities for the rugged young man who was looking for challenges that would engage his curiosity and absorb his energy. The results ranged from his first brush with the world of racing cars to an entry-level job working for his father.

Jack had always been a hard worker. While in grade school, he delivered newspapers from his bicycle to earn a penny a paper. By the time he was eight, he was working part-time for his father and doing odd jobs such as picking up trash and painting for ten cents an hour. Then came World War II, with its shortage of workers as men entered military service, and the motorcycle, which made Jack available for regular work hours after school and during summer recesses.

One memorable job was making cast-iron practice bombs for the Army Air Corps. The process started by packing a mixture of sand and oil into a rack around a wooden mold, then breaking the rack down into halves to remove the mold. Two holes were created from the top, one for receiving the metal and one for gas to escape. Meanwhile, iron was melted over burners in the cupola, where the molten iron reached a temperature of 2,400 degrees. The iron was drained into buckets, carried to the molds, poured down the holes, and allowed to cool. The racks were then broken apart and the practice bombs were taken out and trimmed. In the afternoons, Jack and his co-workers shook out and screened the sand castings so the process could begin again the next day. As Jack later recalled, "there was nothing like working in a foundry to make you appreciate getting cleaned up." [21]

As a wartime teenager, Jack filled gaps in a machine shop and on an assembly line making industrial burners and floor furnaces at a local manufacturer. The opportunity to work with men, use tools, and learn how the component parts of complex machines were designed, fabricated, and assembled was possible due to the early success and perseverance of an up-and-coming local businessman who had believed enough in himself and his chosen city to start a business just as the shadows of the Great Depression were spreading across the land. And this businessman was well-known to Jack; it was his father, John Steele Zink.

In 1929, only a year after Jack was born, John was still working for Oklahoma Natural Gas Company (ONG), a good and growing firm known for treating its workforce well. As a monopoly in Tulsa, Oklahoma City, and other communities, it was regulated by the Oklahoma Corporation Commission, which rewarded the company for customer service, dependability, and efficiency. Innovative sidelines and enterprising ideas unrelated to the core mission of delivering gas to satisfied customers were not part of the corporate culture, and were therefore discouraged.

John, in charge of industrial sales at ONG, could not help being himself. On the job he did what he was told to do, sell natural gas, but he could not help seeing the antiquated boilers and furnaces his customers used to burn the product. He started playing around with different concepts, experimenting with new designs, and eventually came up with a better burner, one that used less fuel, burned more efficiently, and generated more steam with less upkeep. His first "horizontal bi-mix gas burner" was assembled at his home and sold from the trunk of his car. When officials at ONG found out about their employee's innovative moonlighting, they neither embraced it nor used it to their advantage. Instead, they told John

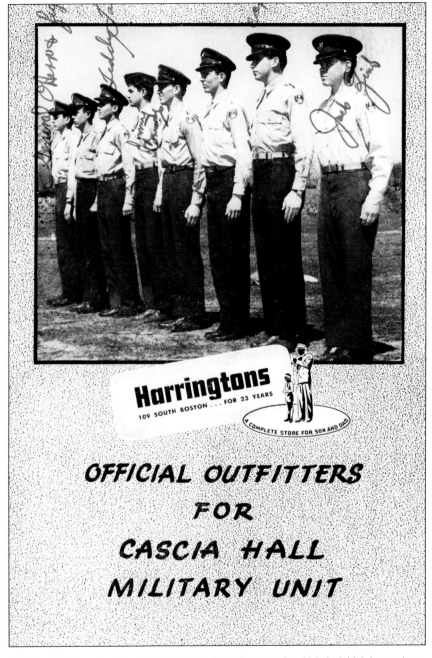

This Cascia Hall yearbook included a page on the cadet corps, in which Jack (right) served as a section leader.

Cable tool drilling rigs needed burners to heat water in the boilers that provided power for drilling. Jack's father, John, invented a better burner in 1929.

to either work exclusively for them, doing only what they told him to do, or he should quit. Believing in his new burner, he chose the latter option. [22]

Although he knew the future of any new business was risky, John was armed with two advantages that gave him the courage to leave a good, steady salary for a fledgling new enterprise. One was his own self-confidence, a combination of personal will and natural optimism forged from life experiences that had steadily progressed from hog farming to college, from entry-level job to director of industrial sales at one of Oklahoma's most prestigious companies. The other advantage that fired his willingness to take a chance was the potential market he saw every day as he dealt with client after client. He did not have to base his expected sales on far away, unfamiliar markets. The business demand for his product was at his fingertips, in Tulsa, Oklahoma, the "Oil Capital of the World."

Tulsa was one of the world's most amazing success stories. Starting as a sleepy Creek Indian trading community at the turn of the century, it became one of the fastest growing cities in the country from 1915 to 1930, with soaring skyscrapers, magnificent mansions, and a workforce that came from around the world with capital, skills, and energy. Every chapter of that story, the buildings, the homes, the growing population, had one thing in common—oil.

The plot of the story opened with a trickle of oil at Red Fork in 1902, but gained momentum with the discovery of the more prolific Glenn Pool in 1905. Tulsa leaders, armed with the closest rail depot to both fields, established their town as the first central nervous system for oil play in the old Indian Territory. With headquarters in Tulsa, oilmen branched out and discovered other fields such as the Greater Osage, Healdton, Three Sands, the Greater Seminole, and one of the most important of them all, Cushing.

The Cushing Field, discovered only thirty miles southwest of Tulsa by "King of the Wildcatters" Tom Slick, started flowing in 1915 just as World War I was sinking into a grinding battle of attrition dependent on overseas shipping, mobility behind the lines, and increased use of mechanized machines of war such as tanks. At home, the recently unveiled Model T was rolling off Henry Ford's assembly lines, putting automobiles within reach of workers and farmers for as little as $400, available on the innovative new installment plan. Both the war effort and the growing number of gas guzzling automobiles created an overnight, burning demand for oil, and the place it came from in 1915 was Cushing.

Cushing was an important outpost for Tulsa's army of drillers and producers, but if the hunt for and production of oil had been the only impact on the host city, the growth would have been short lived, surviving only as long as the derricks went up and the drill pipes hit pay sands. The real impact of the Cushing Field on Tulsa was in the accelerated construction of refineries driven by the growing worldwide demand for gasoline.

John Steele Zink (left) with guests at the plant he built at 44th and S. Peoria in Tulsa.

The first facility to convert crude oil to gasoline and other products in Tulsa was the Humboldt Refinery, built in 1907. A few other refineries followed, but none of them had enough capacity to affect markets or change the flow of crude. That milestone was hit in 1913 when Josh Cosden built his first refinery on eighty acres in the shadow of the city west of the Arkansas River. When the Cushing Field started flowing, Cosden added more units and expanded until his refinery covered more than 600 acres, an area a mile long and a mile wide. With such capacity creating an insatiable appetite for crude oil, producers laid a tangled web of pipelines into Tulsa's refinery district, adding even more incentive to build refineries

HEAT MAKERS

Forced Air Central Heaters

Floor Furnaces

Unit Heaters

Conversion Burners

Burners for:
Refinery Stills
and Furnaces

Gasoline Plant Boilers

Drilling Boilers

Treating Furnaces

Domestic Furnaces

Heating Boilers

Power Boilers

Burners for Air Heaters

DOMESTIC

INDUSTRIAL

COMMERCIAL

4401 South Peoria   Tulsa 1, Oklahoma

and establish company headquarters. By 1928 Tulsa was clearly the "Oil Capital of the World," with twelve refineries and 1,500 companies tied to the oil industry. [23]

Importantly to John Zink, the essential element used at all those refineries was the application of high heat. At its basic level, crude oil is a mixture of many different hydrocarbons, which are molecules made from hydrogen and carbon. In any given sample of crude oil, there may be a few or there may be many different combinations called fractions. Some are light fractions, such as gasses and gasoline, while some are heavy, such as lubricants and asphalt. At a refinery, the objective is to take crude oil, which has little practical use, and break it down into useful products that have value. This conversion is achieved by applying heat to the crude, agitating the molecules, and separating large hydrocarbons into smaller pieces, thus the common term, "cracking."

Working around this industry, John Zink recognized the fundamental challenges facing the refinery owners. They needed high heat in furnaces, as high as 1,500 degrees Fahrenheit, but the burners they used to produce the heat in the furnaces were crude and inefficient. If he could design a burner that burned less fuel, it would save the operator money. If the burner was smaller, it would take up less space and concentrate the heat more evenly. And if the burner was more reliable, it would take less maintenance, and less maintenance meant the furnaces were on line more hours and making more money. It was this market niche, which was underserved and growing, that attracted the attention and creative energy of John Zink. It was this market niche that convinced him to try a new career.

The John Zink Company, launched in 1929, grew steadily despite the widening Depression. In Tulsa John opened a small sales office in the Oklahoma Natural Gas Building, but his burners were cast, assembled, and shipped from a foundry in Sand Springs. To find customers, he drove his Model T into the oil fields, picked up worn-out burners, and delivered those that had been rebuilt. On any given trip he might haul fifteen to twenty units at a time. After only one year, he had enough confidence in

The first building to house the John Zink Company (pages 14 and 15) had been used for circus animals, including elephants. Decades later, Jack could still remember cleaning up the mess they left.

John's full page advertisement (left) in the Tulsa City Directory to promote his product line.

the company that he took out a quarter-page advertisement in the Tulsa City Directory that touted "John Zink Company industrial burners... the Bi-Mix will burn the richest gas with a flameless fire, and will generate more steam with less upkeep than any other burner." The ad included an illustration of the burner and the qualities important to his potential customers, "Atmospheric Injecting, Quick Mixing, and Flameless." [24]

In 1934 John moved the operations to 424 East 4th Street and added a machine shop. A year later, convinced his company would survive, he purchased a ten-acre plot of land south of town, surrounded by cultivated fields near the future intersection of South 44th Street and Peoria. On the property, which was not then in the city limits, there was a two-story frame building that had been used by a circus. One of Jack's first duties, later recalled with vivid disgust, was to clean out the animal waste from the ground floor where the elephants and horses had been wintered. Each year thereafter, John would buy more drill presses, more lathes, and more welding equipment as he subsequently added a machine shop, tin shop, carpenters shop, and pattern shop. [25]

Even as the company moved to the new location in July of 1935, the market for burners was changing. Refineries, like heavy industry in general, suffered from the worldwide economic stagnation as well as overproduction in the oil patch, which drove the price of crude oil to less than a dime a barrel in 1933. Even worse for the John Zink Company, the acknowledged status of Tulsa as the center of the American oil industry began to fade as oil play shifted toward Houston and Los Angeles, where the prolific Permian Oil Basin in West Texas and new fields in Southern California became the new hot spots for land men, drillers, and producers. By 1933, half of all drilling and production hands and one-third of refinery employees in Tulsa were unemployed. Either bankrupt or barely surviving, refinery owners and drillers saw no need for new burners. The John Zink Company would have to find additional markets if it were to survive. [26]

The new market found was the revived home building industry. Across the nation, middle class families secured long term, low interest loans for homes because the Federal Housing Administration, created as one of President Franklin Roosevelt's New Deal agencies in 1934, would guarantee those loans. After years of pent up demand, this secured source of financing ignited a building boom.

Along with the new wave of home building came a growing demand for a relatively new type of heating device, the floor furnace. In areas where natural gas was widely distributed, builders and home owners discovered that floor furnaces, mounted in crawl spaces with grilles at floor level, would use heat induction to provide more heat, more efficiently than the old fashioned open flame area heaters. Builders found that homes equipped with this latest device would sell quicker. Even in older homes, which often were furnished with oil burning boilers and gravity-flow furnaces, there was a demand for conversion to either floor furnaces or natural gas burners. All of this came to the attention of John Zink and his craftsmen who were looking for new applications for their products.

In 1936 John and his crews started experimenting with floor furnaces then on the market. After three years of research, all the while watching industrial sales decline, they came up with a better product, which, according to John, "combined all the good points of competitive furnaces and omitted the bad points." He must have been right. By 1947 the plant on Peoria was producing 2,000 floor furnaces a month, shipping to all forty-eight states and grossing more than $1 million a year. In newspaper articles, John referred to the floor furnaces as "the principal product of the company" and "the golden step" in the early history of the firm. [27]

John did not give up on the industrial burner product line, despite the decline in sales. Instead, he developed new variations that could be applied to a variety of tasks. When America entered World War II, the continued research and development paid off with new industrial sales for burners that could more efficiently produce essential products such as gasoline, toluene, styrene, butadiene, magnesium picric acid, carbon, and anhydrous ammonia. By the end of the war the John Zink Company was producing more than fifty types of burners for industrial use. [28]

In 1946 the foundry building at the Peoria site burned. In its place John built a new, enlarged complex with an office building, storage building, and production plant with 40,000 square feet of open space where 100 craftsmen formed, machined, and welded burners and floor furnaces to the music of Beethoven and Mozart. John, in one interview, said the men liked music, especially at mealtime and just before they finished their day's work. Another benefit enjoyed by the employees was top pay and regular bonuses. One reporter, describing John's management style, said

he was "autocratic and thoughtful, demanding and lavish with praise, kind hearted and hard fisted, and considered an almost perfect boss by those who work for him." [29]

Jack, growing up in the 1930s and early 1940s, was a witness to and sometime partner in this embryonic business growth. Making the experience even more personal and accessible was the fact that his father was a self-contained management team. In numerous articles published in the 1930s and 1940s, John was described as "one of the last of the rugged individualists." One reporter quoted his approach to business: "I've been my own manager, my own banker, my own patent lawyer, and my own engineer. I put up my own buildings with my own money. When I did not have the cash to do what I wanted, I always waited until I got it. I own this business lock, stock, and barrel." For Jack, his father's steady, innovative approach to business, combining courage and caution, would be another lesson learned. [30]

—⟨∞⟩—

The Harley Davidson 45 motorcycle, which made regular work hours possible for the teenager, opened other worlds of opportunity and allowed Jack to follow his own interests separate from family, school, and work. One of those interests was racing.

Jack's love of automobiles and racing can be dated to 1937, when an uncle took the nine-year-old boy to see midget cars race at the Detroit Motor Speedway. The speed, the competition, the adventure of flying around the track to prove who was the best prepared and who was the best driver appealed to the youngster. Back in Tulsa, Jack's interest in racing was cultivated by Ellis Bell, the father of a neighborhood friend and announcer at the Tulsa Fairgrounds Speedway. On Saturday nights each summer until the war began, Jack and his friend would be at the track following their favorite drivers. [31]

Watching race cars was not enough. In 1941 Jack assembled what

John Steele Zink (right) was described by one reporter as "the last of the rugged individualists." He did not bend to other people's expectations of how he should dress, play, or manage his business.

By 1930, Tulsa (facing page) was the financial and industrial center of the Mid Continent Oil Field with 200,000 people and a skyline pierced by skyscrapers (Courtesy Oklahoma Historical Society).

Jack served as business manager of the Cascia Hall school yearbook.

would be the first in a series of cars he would build. It was a simple design, consisting of a two-horsepower engine mounted on a wooden frame built from one-by-twelve inch boards. Without a clutch, the engine was engaged by leaning to the right, which tightened the drive belt enough to go forward. When he wanted to stop, he leaned to the left to loosen the belt. Two years later, west of the John Zink Company plant on Peoria, Jack used his father's tractor to scrape out a one-eighth mile oval dirt track. It was great for riding his motorcycle, but the real fun was driving the family's 1938 Ford Sedan around the track as fast as his fifteen-year-old skills would take him. Then Jack met Felix Graves, a mechanic with a shop at 31ˢᵗ Street and Harvard in Tulsa. [32]

Felix was a car man. He worked on them. He understood them. And he raced them. Before the war, Felix built and drove his own race cars, including a popular new style of open-wheeled racer called midgets. With a seventy-two-inch wheelbase and powerful engine, the mini Indy-style cars were wildly popular with racing crowds and drivers. Felix, a convert to the new style of car, became a regular at the races every weekend. He even built an innovative trailer designed to carry two race cars, one on top of the other, made possible by a swiveled pivot that allowed Felix to tilt the trailer down to load and unload the top car. [33]

Felix became more than just a friend to Jack. He became a mentor. Felix and his wife, Babe, had no children, so they welcomed into their home the eager young man who was not afraid to work and learn. Jack respected Felix's mechanical ability and enjoyed working around the garage and learning about cars. Jack also enjoyed the camaraderie of the local racing regulars who used Felix's shop as an unofficial headquarters and clubhouse. By the time he was a senior in high school, Jack had convinced Felix to help him build his own V8-60 midget racer. [34]

The project was ambitious, given that new parts were nowhere to be found during the war. Under Felix's watchful eye, Jack built the racer from the ground up, using spare parts where possible and scavenging junkyards for other parts that could be shaped and tooled to meet their needs. They welded rails to make the low-slung chassis, then cut and welded ten-gauge sheet metal to form the body, carefully creating "kick ups" so the body would arch up and over the rear axle. During his first year at Oklahoma A&M, Jack took back roads on his motorcycle trips to and from Stillwater to look for parts in farmers' fields. One particular need was a set of twelve-inch brake drums from a Model T that could be modified to make the center part of a racing wheel. For an engine they found and overhauled a Ford flathead V8. For suspension they used leaf springs found in a junkyard. [35]

For two years, Jack worked on the project, carefully balancing the hobby with school, football, family time, and work at the plant. Finally, after investing heart and soul into his creation, the car builder was ready to show it to his father. John, as a protective, supporting parent, reacted with mixed emotions. He was proud of his son, recognizing the time, energy, and creativity that went into the car. He also was concerned about the next step, driving the race car, so he made a deal with his son. He asked, "Jack, if given the opportunity and resources, could you build a better race car?" When Jack said "yes," his father said, "build the best car you can." Unsaid but understood was an agreement that the young car builder would not drive the car himself. With that deal, the John Zink Company began its sponsorship of automobile racing and Jack Zink began an avocation that would lead to the highest victory lanes of success. [36]

The John Zink Company served as a learning laboratory for Jack, who worked with his mind as much as his hands on the production floor.

Into the First Turn

"A winner says 'I'm good, but not as good as I ought to be.'
A loser says 'I'm not as bad as a lot of people.'"

Jack Zink

CHAPTER TWO

Oklahoma A&M in Stillwater was the perfect college for Jack, who mixed studies with a growing role on his John Zink Company race team. While he was in college, Jack (page 22) built and drove stock cars on regional dirt tracks.

In 1913 nationally known driver Joe Nikrent (facing page) brought to Oklahoma the Case he had raced at the Indianapolis 500 (Courtesy Oklahoma Historical Society).

As the summer of 1946 drew to a close, seventeen year old Jack Zink found himself at a crossroads in his young life. Behind were the familiar comforts of home, the bonds of friends and school, and the challenges of hard work and disciplined teamwork at the plant. Ahead were new opportunities that would add to the lessons learned.

At the center of this new chapter in his life was college. Jack chose to attend Oklahoma A&M at Stillwater, Oklahoma, partly because it was only sixty miles west of Tulsa, but more importantly, because it offered one of the nation's top programs in mechanical engineering, a tradition that dated to the school's founding as a land grant institution in 1890. Raised in an industrial plant where craftsmen used tools and ingenuity to develop new products through trial and error, Jack wanted to learn the science and principles behind the way things worked.

When he arrived on the Stillwater campus in September of 1946, Jack was surrounded by thousands of veterans just returning from military service and going to school on the G.I. Bill. The first semester he lived under the football stadium in a crowded room filled with bunk beds for twenty-six students. The second semester he moved into the recently completed Cordell Hall, where he shared quarters with three roommates. By his junior year he lived in a boarding house on the north side of town. [1]

Jack liked the balance he found at A&M. Influenced by his mother, he enjoyed the liberal arts courses that all students took, from history and political science to art and literature. Like his father, he enjoyed courses in mathematics, science, and applied technology. Jack felt at home in Stillwater, with its small scale and strong sense of community where town and gown coexisted seamlessly. Even the student body suited Jack. It reflected Oklahoma, with most of the kids coming from the small towns, farms, and ranches that still dotted the young state.

Oklahoma A&M had fraternities and sororities, but they blended easily into the larger flow of campus life without the stark separations and rivalries found on other, more urban campuses. Although not interested in joining a fraternity, Jack noticed that the Greeks had test banks and study halls, so he organized other "independents" into a study group with their own files of tests and scheduled sessions for book work. By his senior year he was selected a member in the Society of Automotive Engineers, an honorary scholastic fraternity. [2]

Years later Jack would remember Oklahoma A&M fondly. He recalled the many life long friends made on campus, such as King Kirchner, a fellow motorcycle enthusiast and native of Perry who would build Unit Corporation into an international power in the energy industry. Another was Ed Joullian, a classmate who would turn Mustang Fuels into one of the largest natural gas providers in the state. He also remembered his professors, who taught him to predict outcomes based on calculation and measured reasoning. In 1977, when his alma mater inducted him into the Oklahoma State University Engineering Hall of Fame, he would reflect on those memories and the influence that college had on his life. [3]

For Jack Zink, the years from 1946 to 1950 were important, perhaps some of the most important years in his life, but it was not just the college experience, or the education, or the friends. While he enjoyed those parts of his new life, his heart and soul remained true to his first love—car racing—and it was car racing that provided lessons that could not be learned in the classroom.

From 1946 to 1950 Jack spent virtually every weekend and summer working on race cars, hauling race cars, and ultimately, driving race cars. Like college, racing was a new and exciting world, a distinct culture with its own cast of characters and traditions that beat to the rhythms of

Car racing quickly challenged horse racing as the most popular sport in Oklahoma after statehood in 1907. Here, fans watch from the Grandstand at the State Fair of Oklahoma in Oklahoma City (Courtesy Oklahoma Historical Society).

engines and speed. It was a world with its own language, ruled by values shaped through competition and the will to win. To Jack Zink, it was a wonderful world and he was going to be part of it.

Racing culture was as old as the state. The first races in the United States had been staged in 1895, but they were essentially endurance races to see if the newfangled contraptions could get from one city to the next. In 1908, only a year after Oklahoma statehood, two drivers went head to head in such a "race" from Oklahoma City to Kansas City. The distance was 438 miles and the winning time was nineteen hours, forty-two minutes. [4]

The first grand prix type race, held on an enclosed course, was run in 1904. Within the year, race teams led by famous drivers such as Barney Oldfield were barnstorming through Oklahoma, using horse race tracks to display their cars and skills. One such barnstormer was Louis Disbrow,

billed as the "world's circular dirt track racing king," who brought his team of seven cars and five "auto pilots" to the State Fair of Oklahoma in 1913. [5]

According to the press coverage, the top three drivers were record holders. Disbrow, driving a 280-horsepower Jay-Eye-See and the lighter, faster Simplex Zip, had recently broken seven track records set earlier by Barney Oldfield. The most experienced driver was Wild Bill Endicott, driving a car called Tornado, described as "one of the fastest 450-cubic-inch cars in America today." The other record holder was "the flying Californian," Joe Nikrent, driving a Case he had piloted in the most recent Indianapolis 500, already a world famous race at only two years old. For forty percent of the gate and concessions, these auto racing pioneers offered a glimpse of the future to a community accustomed to horses and buggies. [6]

For the next twenty years car racing gradually displaced horse racing

Open wheel racecars make the turn at the State Fair of Oklahoma as they pass one of the exhibition halls built in 1907 (Courtesy Oklahoma Historical Society).

as the premier event at fairs and festivals, anywhere crowds gathered for recreation, but the sport was largely confined to professional drivers and car owners who could afford the high priced racing machines. The State Fair of Oklahoma in Oklahoma City and the Oklahoma State Fair in Muskogee became regular stops on the national circuits, attracting crowds as large as 20,000 to 30,000 a day. There were traditional lap races, novelty events such as "auto polo," and the ultimate survivor spectacles, demolition derbies. In Tulsa, where the Free Fair was organized in 1915, migratory racing teams finally had a place to compete in the "Oil Capital of the World."[7]

During the 1920s and 1930s America became a nation on wheels, thanks in large part to the declining prices of mass production and the ability of working men to keep older cars running. As automobiles became more common and engines grew bigger and more powerful, it was natural that the thrill of speed and the call of competition would draw new converts to racing, first on public roads, then on dirt tracks carved from the prairie grass. Soon, home-grown tracks could be found near towns both large and small, places where local boys could run their cars and test their courage.

By 1938 weekly dirt track racing in Oklahoma was organized and drawing growing crowds. In Oklahoma City a promoter cleared ground for a half-mile track one mile west of Wiley Post Airport, located on the western edge of the city, and announced regular "Junk Car" racing with local drivers. One night during the summer of 1938, a reporter noted that the country racetrack drew twenty cars and staged three events, capped by a feature race of fifty laps. In Tulsa, where golf, baseball, football, sailing, and even polo dominated sports page coverage, reporters rarely recognized the grassroots, recreational sport that was growing in the hinterlands.[8]

The gap between democratic "Junk Car" racing and expensive professional racing such as the Indianapolis 500 was eventually filled by a hybrid of both. It was called midget car racing. In 1933, race promoters in California recognized that the economic grip of the Great Depression was driving down the price they could charge for admission, which in turn reduced the purses they could offer to car owners. What they came up with was a cheaper racecar, a scaled down version of the full sized cars seen at Indy that could be built and maintained on the lower purses. Limited to a seventy-two-inch wheelbase and either a 110-cubic-inch overhead cam four-cylinder engine or a 200-cubic-inch stock-based engine, the lighter, more maneuverable cars created the same excitement and thrills as their larger cousins. A new sport was born.[9]

Midget car racing quickly spread from California to the rest of the nation, pushed forward by two forces. First, the car could be fabricated from spare parts available in almost any community where steel rails, sheet metal, transaxles, suspension systems, and discarded engines—the raw materials for a midget—were cheap and plentiful. Second, the smaller cars could be handled by beginning drivers, offering an irresistible opportunity to brave young men who wanted to learn how to control high-speed vehicles on slippery surfaces. Together, the affordability and accessibility of midgets drew thousands of mechanically minded men to local racing. And as their numbers grew, so did the number of tracks where they could test their machines and skills.

In Oklahoma City, which had long been a regional magnet for racing, the new sport caught on immediately. The first dedicated venue was the 5,175-seat Stockyards Coliseum, built in 1930 in the old National Stockyards district on the southwest side of town, where events on the indoor floor usually featured boxing and wrestling matches, conventions, and auto shows. In 1938 a local promoter familiar with midget racecars installed an oval track in the building to handle the smaller cars. The result was a six-month season of midget car racing from July to December. The last race of the season was typical of the program, with seven events including matched team races, heat races, and a thirty-five-lap feature event.[10]

By 1940 midget car races had come to Tulsa. As in Oklahoma City, where the purses never grew large enough to attract the nation's top drivers, the cars and drivers were largely from the local area with a few touring veterans working their way across the country to pay for expenses. One of the local boys trying his hand at the new style of racing was Felix Graves, owner of a garage at 31st and Harvard, who had become an understanding mentor to the young Jack Zink.

Like most mechanics of his day, Felix learned to work on cars through a combination of aptitude and necessity. There were no computers, no electronics, and no sophisticated fuel injection systems that required technical training or certification. For ex-farm boys like Felix, working on cars took a few tools and a willingness to tear into the mechanical beast, whether it was grinding valves and rebuilding carburetors or straightening drive shafts and dented fenders. These skills transferred easily to building the new midget racecars.

Through 1940 and 1941, before Jack was even a teenager, Felix became a regular at the local track. He built his first car with a flat-head Ford engine, then followed with a second car and his innovative double-decker trailer that could haul both. For part time racing converts like Felix, the track became a home away from home, a place where he and his friends could gather once a week and compare their mechanical creations, test their driving skills, and have a good time. Even the spectators had

access to this new "racing" culture. There was a thin line between drivers, car owners, and the loyal crowds who came out to cheer them on, which created a club-like atmosphere that pulled people together and forged bonds that would last a lifetime.

Felix, who was well liked, became a central character in the Tulsa world of racing. He met other drivers from surrounding towns, like Chickasha-native Buzz Barton, a large, outgoing mountain of a man whose aggressive driving style and ever-present cigar clenched between his teeth made him a crowd favorite. He met car owners such as M.A. Walker, an electrical contractor from Oklahoma City whose love of the sport seemed

Buzz Barton in the Kurtis Kraft midget racecar John and Jack assembled from a kit in 1947.

ARROWHEAD SPEEDWAY
HOUSTON, TEXAS
THURSDAY

TO INDY AND BEYOND: THE LIFE OF RACING LEGEND JACK ZINK

to have no bounds. And he met an eager teenage boy who had access to the racing club through his friend's father, Ellis Bell, who was the announcer at the track. That car-crazy kid was Jack Zink.

The friendship with Felix Graves led to the story of Jack's homemade midget racer and the fateful day when Jack's father, John, inspected the car and agreed to bankroll a first class racecar sponsored by the John Zink Company. And in 1946 a first class racecar meant one thing to John, Jack, and Felix—a Kurtis-Kraft midget.

―⚬⁄⚬⁄⚬―

Frank Kurtis, whose star was just beginning to rise in the annals of racecar history, was the son of Croatian immigrants. His father earned his living first as a blacksmith in the coal mining towns of Utah, Wyoming, and Colorado, then as an auto mechanic in Southern California, where the family moved in 1918. Growing up around blacksmith shops and garages, young Frank learned to work with tools and metal, skills that helped him get a job at the Don Lee Coach and Body Works Company in 1922. There, he joined a team of craftsmen and artists who customized luxury cars for flamboyant Hollywood stars such as Tom Mix.[11]

Over the next two decades, Kurtis honed his skills in the fertile fields of Southern California car culture. Down the street on Long Beach Avenue were the shops of Harry Miller, the greatest racecar builder in the world, who had taken Indianapolis and the racing world by storm with his innovative, front wheel drive car designs. Closer to home within the Don Lee Coach team was Harley Earl, who later moved to Detroit where he became the key designer behind the emergence of General Motors as the world's most stylish auto builder. Earl, who remembered the promising young Kurtis, offered him a job in Detroit. Frank, more interested in custom car design and racecars, turned him down.

In 1936, with his own shop, Kurtis worked on his first midget racecars. Initially, it was repair work, which allowed him to see how others were building the popular new style of car. Then he took on the challenge of building a midget from the frame up. Adapting the aerodynamic lines of the Art Deco era, his first creation was so sleek and beautiful it was called the "Jewel Box."

By its second year of racing, the John Zink Race Team had two cars on the Midwest Midget circuit. Here, one of the cars waits for a race in Houston.

Jimmy Reece, the son of a racecar driver, became one of Jack's best friends and one of his most talented drivers.

That first car earned him $600, approximately $9,000 in 2008 dollars. [12]

By 1940 Kurtis annually followed his clients to Indianapolis and the world famous race held every Memorial Day. There, he met other car builders, saw different design concepts, and witnessed what worked well and what did not. Then came America's entrance into World War II, which closed the tracks but did not interrupt Kurtis's learning curve. Turning from cars to aviation contracts, Kurtis and his shop workers learned to work with ground breaking aviation designs and high performance metals and plastics. Each new innovation used to create lighter and faster airplanes would later be adapted to racecar design. [13]

In 1945, as the war was coming to an end, Kurtis combined his accumulated knowledge of cars and aviation technology to design a new midget racecar, the first purpose-built racecar created for quantity production. He built the frames from aviation-quality 4130 chrome molybdenum tubing welded with steel rod. The high tech tubing was both lighter and stiffer than the traditional channel-shaped frame rails long used for car chassis, which reduced the weight of the car and allowed Kurtis to use an innovative torsion bar suspension system that kept the tires of the car on the racing surface more effectively, which in turn improved traction and allowed drivers to power their cars through turns. He designed the cars to run with either a standard Ford engine or the innovative new four-cylinder Offenhauser. Painted, chromed, and equipped with the Offy and a 12-gallon fuel tank, the new race-ready midget cost $5,000. The trailer, custom made for the car, was an additional $500. [14]

As word of the new design spread through the racing world, Kurtis quickly received ten orders for completed midgets. That fall and winter of 1945, he and his crews built the frames, formed the aluminum bodies, and added stock parts such as axles, transmissions, and wheels. A few of the cars hit the tracks in 1946 with spectacular results. The car was fast. It hugged the track. And it was dominant, turning journeymen drivers into overnight stars. The result was a backlog of orders that reached six months by May of 1946. Soon, the Kurtis shop was turning out a car a day. [15]

To expand sales, Kurtis offered kits that could be ordered at a cheaper price and assembled by the new owners. In February of 1946, he ran an advertisement in the *National Speed Sport News* announcing that he

Jack receives a winning trophy after one of his many victories driving the '37 Ford stockcar.

would take orders for both kits and cars. According to the ad, the Kurtis-Kraft was "ultra modernistic," with a "stream lined body style…jig built with all parts replaceable and interchangeable." A reporter writing in the same magazine predicted that the car "bids fair to become the sensation of the decade in chassis design and body style." It was an accurate prediction. Within the next year Kurtis sold seventy-six kits to car owners who wanted the best equipment. One of those buyers was a college kid in Oklahoma, Jack Zink.[16]

Jack, although only eighteen years old at the time, was surprisingly well prepared for the venture into the world of midget car racing. At his father's industrial plant, he had learned to work with metal and tools. He knew how mechanical devices worked and the importance of careful calibrations and fittings. And he knew how to work on cars and engines, a process that had begun on the old Model T truck parked in his family's back yard and expanded through his fascination with motorcycles and homemade cars. Just as importantly, he knew how to work within a team, which in the world of racing included mechanics, drivers, track officials, and competitors.

Solidly behind him was his father, John Steele Zink, who had both the financial resources and the vision to invest several thousand dollars in what initially looked to others like a hobby. John recognized the passion his son had for the sport, and he wanted to encourage him, but he also saw the venture as a way to promote his products, John Zink burners and floor furnaces. The company name on the side of a winning car would be a great way to advertise among the public six months out of the year, seven nights a week. There also was the possibility of getting some of his investment back by winning purses. In 1947 Oklahoma driver, "Tiny" Ted Parker, won $6,000 at the Oklahoma City track alone.

At their side was Jack's long time friend, Felix Graves, who knew cars inside and out and understood the ways of the racing world. In addition to his mechanical ability, Felix provided an essential asset—experience—and he was willing to share it with his young protégé. He also brought to the team the advice and encouragement of the local racing crowd, including the cigar-chewing Buzz Barton, a skilled mechanic and body worker who had

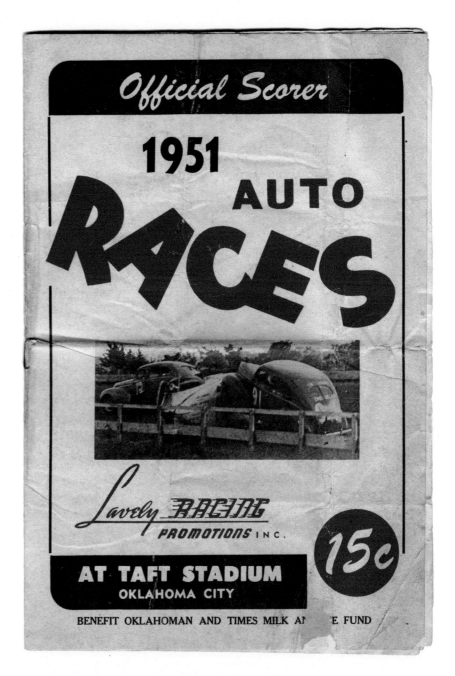

By 1951 Jack was one of the most successful drivers on regional dirt tracks. He was a regular at Taft Stadium in Oklahoma City.

TO INDY AND BEYOND: THE LIFE OF RACING LEGEND JACK ZINK

raced before the war and was looking for a mount to get him to the checkered flag. An experienced mechanic later would say that the only two things Buzz could not weld were a "broken heart and the break of day."

With Felix's experience, Jack's tenacity, and John's resources, the ambitious young team ordered the dominant midget racecar in the world, a Kurtis-Kraft in kit form ready to be assembled. The kit, which included the best Offenhauser on the market, cost $1,165 for the chassis and $2,000 for the engine. As it went together, the team marveled at the engineering of the tube frame, the molded aluminum panels, the plexiglass windshield, the aircraft quality fasteners, and the torsion bar suspension. The engine, a thing of beauty to Jack, roared to life after it was installed. Then came the paint scheme, blaze red with white lettering, telling the world that this car, the Zink Racing Team entry, was the "John Zink Special." By the spring of 1947 the car was ready for the track.[17]

The hottest regional track for midgets at the time was Taft Stadium in Oklahoma City. Built as a WPA project for the Oklahoma City Public Schools during the Great Depression, it was leased and adapted to racing in 1946 by O.D. and Ray Lavely, two promoters who were nationally known in racing circles. The quarter mile dirt track was perfect for the midgets, which could accelerate quickly on the short straight-aways and power through the tight turns. That first year, so they would not interfere with high school football games over the weekend, races at Taft Stadium were held on Monday nights.[18]

Jack entered his new Offy-powered Kurtis-Kraft at the Taft Stadium track for its inaugural run. That first night, running against cars powered mostly by Fords, Buzz drove the Zink Special to a first place finish in the feature race. Despite the initial success, Jack later would remember that first campaign as a learning experience, which included a major setback when Buzz skidded and wrecked as he took a turn at the State Fairgrounds track. Buzz hauled Jack's pride and joy, the bright red Kurtis-Kraft, to California for repairs, and while he was there ran a few races against some of the best cars and drivers in the world. The learning curve also included a race at Soldier Field in Chicago. In Oklahoma, track officials started the slower cars in front and the faster cars at the back. At the Chicago race,

Lloyd Ruby and Jimmy Reece were Jack's primary drivers on the Midwest Midget circuit that included tracks in Houston, Dallas, Oklahoma City, Tulsa, Wichita, and Kansas City.

there were no "slower" cars. All were fast and highly competitive. By the fall of 1947 the John Zink Special was back on Oklahoma tracks and learning to win.[19]

The 1948 season, which stretched from April to September, was both the Zink team's break out year and the peak of popularity for midget car racing. With crowds of 6,000 to 10,000, typical purses rose to $3,000 and more on circuits that sprung up in California, Washington, Colorado, Texas, Oklahoma, Missouri, Illinois, Indiana, Michigan, New York, New Jersey, New England, and Virginia. For local drivers, the Southwest Championship Circuit went from Kansas City on the north to Houston on the south.

Like the money and crowds, the competition was bigger and better as well. Regional races often drew forty entries, with as many as twenty cars powered by expensive Offy engines. Among the drivers were newcomers such as Lloyd Ruby out of Wichita Falls, Texas, driving the newest $7,000 Kurtis-Kraft, and veterans such as Rabbit Musick, who had won the 1947 inaugural race at Taft Stadium. The growing purses also attracted national champions such as Mack Hellings, who had won the tough West Coast title in 1947.[20]

A typical race card on the circuit started with time trials about 6:30 pm, which established the important starting order for the races that followed. Usually, the two fastest cars were rewarded with a two-car trophy dash, followed by three eight-lap heat races with the top finishers moving onto the feature race. Occasionally, while the qualifiers put the finishing touches on their cars, promoters threw in a Class B race of "Junk Cars" with eight-cylinder engines, and even Class C jalopies with six-cylinder engines. The race card always ended with a sweepstakes feature, usually a twenty-lap race for the biggest share of the purse.[21]

The Zink team, with a solid year of experience behind them, started the season with dramatic flair. Buzz won the first three feature races, all held in Tulsa and Wichita, pulling in an average of $300 to $600 in winnings each time he took the checkered flag. Soon, reporters peppered their articles with descriptions of Buzz, calling him "nervy," "undaunted and popular," and "the best crowd pleaser with his wild-man driving and big black cigar." Unlike later NASCAR races, where drivers would become faceless numbers hidden behind steel and safety equipment, midget car drivers sat high out of their small cars separated from the fans only by helmets and goggles.[22]

A good example of the Zink team's dominance that magical year was the May 18, 1948, program at the Oklahoma State Fairgrounds raceway, which had replaced Taft Stadium as the premier venue in race-crazy Oklahoma City. In front of 6,958 spectators, Buzz "swept the card" when he drove the #2 Zink midget to victory in the time trials, his heat race, and the five mile feature race. Out of the $2,874 purse, the John Zink Special earned $567. [23]

Jack spent the summers of 1948 and 1949 as the team mechanic on the road. Driving a DeSoto coupe and pulling a trailer with the racecar, he and the team drivers started each week racing at the track in Kansas City, followed by overnight trips to Muskogee on Monday, Houston on Tuesday, Dallas on Wednesday, Oklahoma City on Thursday, Tulsa on Friday, and Wichita on Saturday. The routine was to race in the evening, drive through the night, and work on the car the next day until time for the races. The teamwork continued even on the road at night. When the partner riding shotgun noticed the driver getting drowsy, his duty was to reach over the wheel and turn off the lights. For the driver, the rude awakening of keeping the car and trailer on the road while trying to get the lights back on produced a surge of adrenalin, which helped get the team to the next town.[24]

Encouraged by the early success, the Zink team bought another Kurtis-Kraft Offy from an owner in Indiana. Billy Cox, one of Jack's high school and college friends, went with him to pick up the car. Without returning to Tulsa, the two teenagers drove straight to San Antonio, Texas, for a 500-lap race with a $5,000 purse, which included $1,000 for the winner of the feature. Jack's father, John, for some reason did not trust the promoter of the race, so he told his son to make sure the prize money was in escrow. Jack, following through on his father's advice, confronted the promoter when he registered the car. "Don't worry," said the older man, "I've got the money." When Jack persisted, the promoter called to his wife in the stands, who walked up with diamonds draped around her neck and rings dripping from her fingers. "I've got enough money in those jewels to buy the whole pack of cars here tonight," he said. Jack, still unconvinced, nevertheless unloaded and prepared to race.

With Buzz at the wheel, the new #3 John Zink Special won the time

trials, started on the front row, and took the checkered flag after 250 miles of hard driving. When Jack went to pick up the winning purse, he got a check for $400, less than half of what had been promised. As it turned out, the promoter had the money, but the IRS showed up first and claimed it for back taxes. For Jack, it was another victory, another lesson.[25]

With two cars on the circuit, Jack started experimenting with other drivers, each of whom brought their own skills and tendencies. Among them were Marcel St. Criq, followed by Jud Larson, a native of Austin, Texas. By the end of the season, Buzz was the Oklahoma State Champion, followed by Jud in 6th place. Finishing one place ahead of Jud was Cecil Green, a native of Houston, Texas, who drove a Kurtis-Kraft Offy for the M.A. Walker team out of Oklahoma City. Far back in the standings was Oklahoma City teenager, Jimmy Reece, a rookie driver chasing the faster Offys in a Ford. [26]

The 1949 season opened badly for the Zink Race Team. The campaign started in April with one car driven by Buzz and the other by Tommy Vardeman, a native of Tulsa who had driven a Ford the previous year. On one trip to San Antonio, Tommy in the #2 car had the second best time trial, but spun out in the two-car, four-lap trophy dash, then ran last in the four-car, eight-lap heat race. His bad luck continued in the 100-lap feature when he ran slowly and spun out on the ninety-seventh lap. Buzz did a little better, sixth in the time trials, winner of his heat race, but in the feature he had a wreck on the second lap and bent a radius rod in the front end. Buzz and Jack straightened the rod, but lost two laps. The rest of the race he lapped every car once and passed eleven of the sixteen cars a second time to come in sixth. For the night, the team won a paltry $100 for both the cars and the drivers. [27]

In June of 1949 Buzz left the team and was replaced by Cecil Green, a Houston chauffeur renowned for his fearlessness on the track. By July, the other driver, Tommy Vardeman, was leading the Southwest AAA Midget Circuit point standings by an unprecedented margin, but then he, too, left the team. With only one driver and two cars, Jack went with Green as his only driver, alternating cars each night and working on the car not running. Success followed success and Green captured the Southwest Championship after Jack returned to college that fall.

John and Jack kept Midget race cars on the track even after the sport of midget car racing peaked in the early 1950s.

After graduating from college in the spring of 1951, Jack traveled with the race team again, serving as chief mechanic and team leader. For drivers, he chose veteran Bud Camden from Wichita Falls, Texas, and took a gamble on the rookie from Oklahoma City, Jimmy Reece, who had been driving Fords, and whose father had raced cars before the war and currently owned the Cushman motorcycle dealership in Oklahoma City. The chemistry of the trio clicked. Reece was high point man in several cities on the circuit, and in a 500-lap race on the half-mile track in Oklahoma City, he placed second in a star-studded field, which included drivers such as Bill Vukovich, Johnnie Parsons, and Johnnie Tolan. Later that year, their success continued with Reece winning the 1951 Southwest Championship after the team finished first and second at a 600-lap event in Oklahoma City.

Despite such success, the Zink team gradually eased away from full time midget racing, which was suffering from a number of problems. One was too much racing. The sudden popularity of midgets from 1947 to 1949, a time when Americans were looking for a diversion from the sacrifices of war, led to too many tracks, too many race cards, and too many high priced, high powered cars. The market was simply oversold.

Another problem was safety. As crowds grew, purses grew, and as competition intensified, drivers went faster and took greater risks. The result was a growing number of deadly wrecks in a sport that resisted even the most basic safety precautions such as roll bars. The public reacted by staying away and racing officials reacted by shutting down the tracks.

Many tracks across the country that had previously made money suddenly closed. One such closure was at the Tulsa Fairgrounds Raceway, which cancelled its weekly racing program prior to the opening of the 1949 season. At the Kurtis-Kraft factory in Los Angeles, the sad condition of the sport was painfully clear; only one midget racecar was sold in 1950.

Jack would keep the midget cars running for several more years, and he would even build a new midget in the late 1950s, but never again would the team participate in a seven-night-a-week circuit. Instead, the midgets were usually kept closer to home, running in mixed car racing programs that included at best a single race for the faster cars. Typical was a stock car race program in Oklahoma City that included a 500-lap midget race

After graduating from Oklahoma A&M, Jack served as a sales engineer for John Zink Company, working with clients and developing combustion solutions around the world.

with proceeds dedicated to the Milk and Ice Fund. Jimmy Reece drove the Zink Special to a second place finish. The next year promoters in Tulsa put together a stock car program that included a 200-lap feature for midgets, again with Jimmy coming in second. But these races were the exception to the rule. Midget car racing was in decline and the Zink Racing Team would have to look elsewhere for new challenges. For Jack, backing away from racing was not an option; what he needed was something new, something that would fit within the changed circumstances of his life. [28]

—◦◦◦—

In the spring of 1951, Jack was at another crossroads in his young life. He was about to begin his career as the only "sales engineer" for the John Zink Company. The title given to his job reflected what his father expected of Jack. He was to represent the company across the country, wherever burners were needed, and he was to work within the Zink research team to develop new products in the process. One letter, written to Jack in the spring of 1951, described the pressure on the young college graduate.

The letter, written by a company executive, started with news of the race team, but quickly got to business: "the company continues to rock along at the low-low...no orders of any kind...one came in this morning from John A. Dodd for one pilot at $12.75 net...not much butter on our bread at that rate." Jack, who was attending a technical seminar in New York, was told to call C.F. Canney, director of the Tar Products Division of Koppers Products Company; then he was to "move to the Warren Job and thence to Youngstown to fix up that job." The writer adds a note that "Mr. Zink says for you to be sure and write to him every day...that's the only way he can tell if you are earning him any money. He also says to remind you how much money you are costing him and be sure and not overlook the museums, libraries, institutions of learning as well as smoke stacks." [29]

Jack was up to the challenge. He was young, single, and armed with a natural confidence backed by a combination of practical experience in the plant and a first class engineering degree earned at a respected applied science university. On the one hand, like his more senior mentors at the

Burners of all kinds, from floor furnaces to industrial burners and flares of all sizes, such as the small one shown, made the John Zink Company one of the fastest growing industrial firms in the region from 1950 to 1970.

plant, he had worked around machinery long enough that he instinctively understood how one part worked with another, how one material reacted to another, and how observation could be used to detect success or understand failure. On the other hand, he was a man fascinated by the world of numbers, a world he was beginning to master.

This combination of assets, both practical and theoretical, filled a growing need at the John Zink Company as post-war competition and regulatory standards pushed industry to new levels of technical sophistication. Early burners had been designed for the simple task of combusting fuel and transferring energy to the application of heat. With plentiful fuel, little competition, and virtually no environmental protections, quantity was more important than quality. Whether the combustion process generated vapors, liquids, or particulates, the rule was make your product as fast as possible, forget about the waste emissions, and bank the profits.

By the 1940s this formula for success was changing. First was the growing demand for technical efficiency. In the world of combustion, that meant greater "control" of the heat application. Variables included type and mixture of fuel, combustion chamber geometry, thermal input sizes, heat transfer demands, heat release and turndown, firing position, shape of the flame, and ignition type. Pre-mixed air and fuel created shorter and more intense flames; diffusion-mixed flames using raw fuel created longer flames and lower temperature hot spots. Burners ranged from conventional fan-shaped and flat flames to wall-fired and radiant wall burners. Even the materials used for the component parts of burners grew ever more complex, with specific uses for carbon steel, cast iron, cast steel, stainless steel, brass, and ceramic fiber. Then there was the new world of environmental protection.

Whereas greater efficiency, safety, and profitability were market driven, environmental safeguards against hazardous emissions were governmental mandates. Prior to 1947, it was industry practice around the world to vent unburned hydrocarbons into the air, whether it was a power plant, a chemical processing plant, or an oil refinery. Gradually, the federal government set standards and industry had to respond.

Jack developed the first test furnace in the combustion industry (facing page), giving the John Zink Company the ability to design and test burners under the controlled conditions of the plant in Tulsa. One of the fastest growing segments of the combustion equipment business was the design and installation of flares (right).

This created new opportunities for the John Zink Company in products that would still be used around the world in the twenty-first century (although in more technically advanced ways). Flares were employed to safely burn the waste gasses that were previously vented, and were typically large, elevated burners capable of handling a wide range of compositions and quantities of waste gasses, most often from the oil refining process, sometimes in very large amounts and with little advance warning. Appearing something like a large mechanical candle at the top of a very tall stack, their flame in the early days was most often visible and in many cases produced unsightly smoke, as the combustion occurred directly in the atmosphere at the top of the stack. Incinerators, on the other hand, were fully enclosed vessels which used a burner to combust more hazardous waste gasses – or liquids – usually in a steady, predictable flow in a controlled environment within the vessel.

Early flares posed a growing list of challenges, from igniting the flare to burning the waste gasses in a safe and controlled manner, at extremely high temperatures. Reflecting the lack of sophistication to meet such challenges in those early days, some companies ignited flares by hoisting oily, burning rags over the top of the stack, while others shot flaming arrows over the stack. In 1949, the John Zink Company invented the first pilot to light and continuously burn vented gas from a flare stack. What followed was an endless cycle of increased safety and efficiency, with a better understanding of variables such as flow rate, gas composition and temperature, utility costs and availability, safety standards, and environmental requirements.[30]

All of these demands, from greater technical efficiency to greater control over processes, posed new challenges to the way the John Zink Company developed and supported its products. Prior to the 1950s, burners were manufactured at the Zink plant based on what had worked before. When sales representatives in New York, Los Angeles, or Houston sold new burners to new customers, the process was to get specifications from the end user, say a refinery or a boiler operator, and adjust the burner design in the customer's plant using practical experience and trial and error. A new burner would be made, shipped to the customer, installed,

John Zink Company burners were used around the world in industrial heaters and furnaces such as the one shown (left). As a trained engineer, (facing page) Jack had the advantage of solving problems both in the field and at the plant.

and tested on site. If it did not work as expected, another round of experimentation would begin until the desired results were met. Jack led the team that changed the cumbersome process.

Jack knew how many variables had to be considered for a good burner design. With his formal training, he could measure and predict performance through mathematical calculations and theoretical analysis. With his practical experience, he knew firsthand how metals, fuels, and airflow reacted under certain conditions. This combination of education and experience gave him the confidence to explore uncharted waters, to analyze a problem and search for the best solutions through the research team.

Jack recognized other problems in the way new burners were developed. First was profitability. It was inefficient to develop a new burner in the plant, ship it to a site for installation, and then test it to see if it worked. If it needed adjustments, it had to be disassembled, shipped back to the plant, and the entire process repeated until a solution was found. The second problem was safety for his team members. The nature of burners was dangerous, whether in refineries cracking hydrocarbons or in plants firing boilers. Temperatures as high as 2,000 degrees, superheated fluids, and dripping oil put engineers in harm's way every time they had to squeeze into tight places to install or test new equipment. And finally, there was the problem of marketability. The old way to sell new products was to convince a customer that the company could build a burner for their particular need. The only sales tools were the pitch and the reputation of the company. There was nothing to see. There had to be a better way.

In 1951 Jack designed and worked with craftsmen at the plant on Peoria Avenue in Tulsa to build the first test furnace that would help solve each of these problems. It was a ten-feet-wide by fourteen-feet-long box within a box, with an outside wall, an inside wall, and a reservoir of water to remove the heat. A burner under development could be installed in the simulated furnace and tested under close observation. Did the burner light correctly and burn with a stable and controlled flame? Was the flame shaped in a way that it created the greatest possible heat transfer without risking contact with the process tubes? Did the airflow and fuel mix in an efficient manner that would conserve the fuel oil or gas? Were access and

By the mid-1950s Jack (left) spent an average of 200 days a year on the road working for the John Zink Company. With increasing sales to industry, the plant on S. Peoria (facing page) expanded.

line of sight to valves and pilots adequate for efficient operation and safe repairs? Whereas before Jack had to guess at these solutions and test in the field under the critical eyes of clients, with a test furnace he could calculate solutions and check them in the controlled conditions of the John Zink Company plant.[31]

Test burners and applied engineering opened new markets for the John Zink Company, anywhere concentrated heat was needed to convert the molecular form of one compound to another, whether it was oil to gas or toxic emissions to harmless vapor. One such challenge was a Mobil Oil Company refinery in East St. Louis, where a 150-foot flare stack was billowing dark clouds of unburned hydrocarbons into the environment. Jack pulled together a team to find a way to create a smokeless flare to solve the problem. They took measurements, calculated ways to convert the noxious gasses to harmless gasses, and made drawings to get the shop crews working on a new combustion solution.

The critical feature of the design was the introduction of steam injection around the perimeter of the tip of the flare. As waste gasses were discharged from the flare stack, they were injected with steam to improve mixing of the surrounding air and hydrocarbons, thus promoting smokeless combustion. The flare burners were fabricated and tested successfully in the plant, then shipped and installed. Then came the day for the first field test. With a crowd of Mobil engineers looking on, Jack pushed the button to ignite the pilot but nothing happened. He pushed it again, but they could neither see anything nor hear anything. The only option was to climb the 150-foot tower and do a visual inspection. Fifty years later Jack would remember that fifteen-story climb up a ladder with no safety net. He pulled himself up the ladder, one shaky step at a time, until he was only about twenty feet from the top. Then he discovered what was wrong. The design worked too well for them to see any smoke or even hear the roar of the flame from the ground. It was working perfectly, a new smokeless flare that did exactly what his clients needed. [32]

Jack's technical innovations, combined with his father's business skills, helped the company grow in the 1950s. From fewer than twenty employees when Jack graduated from high school, the plant grew to more than 300 workers by the end of the decade. For Jack, the success meant increasing pressure to be everywhere, seeing clients, producing new designs, and working with the guys at the plant building and testing burners and flares. It also kept him on the road at least 200 days a year. Although single and footloose, something had to give, and that something was the regular racing circuits he had enjoyed while in college. Taking its place was an emerging new type of racing, stock cars.

—◦◦◦—

Originally called "junk cars" or "jalopies," stock cars were American production passenger vehicles modified for racing. The popularity of stockcars was easy to understand. On the supply side, promoters liked stockcars because the purses could be smaller and still attract car owners who had very little invested, unlike midget car owners who had as much as $7,000 in each vehicle. On the demand side, stock cars had more "personality" for general audiences. Whereas midget races increasingly pitted look-alike cars that differed only in paint schemes and drivers, stock cars included a wide range of bodies and engines. To some, midget racing had become an expensive, high-bred, high-risk sport with professional drivers, while stock cars emerged as a safer, mongrelized common man's hobby with your next door neighbor at the wheel. Then, there was the excitement of the rising new sport.

The thrill of racing was captured by a brave reporter from Tulsa who rode with the hard charging driver, Jimmie Reece:

> Ollie Goodridge, the starter, came along and told me not to stick my head or arms out of the window, unless I wanted to lose one or the other. We started last in an 18-car pack. Stan Schoenberg was on our left. Charlie Lutkie was immediately in front of us and Bobby Laden was beside him. We were off at 9:40. Going into the second curve on the first lap, a big hole suddenly opened up in the board fence in front of us. Three cars tried to crowd through it. One bounced back in front of us, but Reece curved around it and the accident was behind us.

In the early 1950s, while most of his time was spent on the road working with clients, Jack found time on weekends to race on dirt tracks in Oklahoma.

Reece approaches curves at high speed, between 50 and 60, then brakes the car for a second. Unlike a lot of drivers who slow down going around the curve, he steps on the gas and drives three-fourths of the arc...the car responds to his foot. We'd weave in and out of the snarling traffic until we came to daylight, and then the car would almost fly up to the next auto Reece wanted to pass. He passed all of them, save Lutkie who won the race. [33]

The lure of this new sport attracted Jack Zink. This time, though, he wanted to drive. Since he was fourteen years old he had wanted to go fast. First came the family car on the homemade track at the plant, followed by the motorcycle and his "Daredevil's Club." Midget cars had been tempting, but the risk involved and his father's caution had kept him in the team leader's role. Stock cars, though, were slower and safer, plus they were cheaper to build and simpler to maintain. Less money, less time, plus safer driving meant Jack could finally buckle into the driver's seat.

For his first stockcar, Jack purchased a 1937 Ford sedan, a powerful and popular production car that had been selected as the first fleet vehicle by the newly formed Oklahoma Highway Patrol. To get the old car race-ready, Jack broke out the glass, installed safety glass windshields, and removed sharp objects. He installed roll bars, welded the doors shut, and rolled the fender edges so they would not rip into the tires after collisions. Then he tore out the interior trim, bought a surplus aviator's bucket seat for $10, and welded it to the floor. With seat belts and a padded steering wheel column, the #45 "John Zink Central Heating Units" stockcar was ready to roll. [34]

Jack's first race did not go as planned. Driving on his home track in Tulsa where everyone knew him, he was both nervous and anxious to do well. He got the car started and moved into line, which was a good beginning, but when he saw the green flag, his adrenaline kicked in and he jumped on the gas. Going into the first turn he tapped the brakes and started powering into the curve, but instead of following the other cars around the turn, he felt the driver-side wheels leaving the track. Before he could recover, the car was on its side and he was out of the race. For the appreciative crowd, it was another crash to applaud; for Jack, it was an embarrassing beginning. [35]

Jack did not give up. Instead, he bought two battered Ford coupes to replace the larger sedan and started getting them race-ready for himself and his stable of drivers. During that first season of 1950, team veteran Buzz Barton usually drove one car while Jack "the rookie" drove the other. Although he did not get to race every week because of his budding new business career, Jack raced often that first summer and developed an aggressive driving style, demonstrated clearly at an early race in Oklahoma City. Buzz set the best one-lap qualifying time of 19.17 seconds, followed by Jack who came in second at 19.87. In their heat, Buzz again came in first, with Jack fourth. But in the feature, a 100-lap, twenty-five-mile race, the tables were turned. In a field of twenty-three cars, Buzz started on the pole and led the race for four laps, when, as one reporter said, "Jack whizzed past Buzz on the fifth." The rookie kept the lead and won by a half lap with a time of 32 minutes, 27 seconds. [36]

On another night of racing, Jack got tangled up with popular driver Lloyd Ruby in their heat race. Ruby landed in the infield while Jack limped in on a flat tire. Forced into the twelve-lap consolation race, Jack started in eighteenth place but drove hard to come in second, good enough to get into the twenty-five-lap feature. Again, Jack started back in the pack, with seventeen drivers between him and the checkered flag. With a good car and plenty of muscle under the hood, he worked his way up, one car at a time, until he took the lead on lap fifteen. He kept the pedal down and won the race in record time, nine minutes, four seconds, breaking the old twenty-five-lap record of nine minutes, sixteen seconds. [37]

By 1952 Jack had emerged as one of the hottest drivers in the state. In a profile published in the racing magazine, *Pit Chatter*, the reporter wrote: "Jack likes to win. He gives every race everything he has. It is always clean, fair competition and he's not in the habit of driving right over the car in front of him, which seems to be the popular thing around here lately. In last week's Australian Pursuit he proved he won't be pushed around and can take care of himself...however, he won't ever start the rough stuff." According to the reporter, Jack was "about the best known name in the circuit right now" and "there are more Zink fans than anti-Zink." To back up his assessment, the writer listed Jack's recent accomplishments

Rollovers (facing page) were common sights on the quarter-mile and half-mile dirt tracks where stock cars accelerated in the straight-a-ways, powered into the curves, and banged into each other looking for an advantage.

INTO THE FIRST TURN

Jack (center) with good friend and chief mechanic, Dennie Moore (left) and racing pal and principal driver in the early 1950s, Jimmy Reece.

on the track, including two grand slams (a win in the heat, trophy dash, and feature the same night), three consecutive feature victories in Tulsa, four consecutive feature victories in Oklahoma City, and winning purses in Cushing, Miami, Muskogee, and Enid, Oklahoma.[38]

Unwilling to give up driving even though he was increasingly busy with the John Zink Company, Jack found a new team member for support and mechanical work, a man who would become in effect a partner in the Zink Racing Team. That man was Dennis Moore, better known in racing circles as Dennie.

A native of Iowa, Dennie moved to Oklahoma with his family at the age of four in 1929. He grew up in Oklahoma City, attended Central High School, and joined the Army Air Corps during World War II, making twenty-six missions as a gunner in a B-29. As a kid, Dennie hung around a neighbor's auto repair shop and took all the course work he could in auto mechanics. After the war he went to work for the Oklahoma Transportation Company as a bus mechanic, then moved to Fred Jones Ford as a mechanic in 1954. In the meantime, he attended the stock car races at Taft Stadium and started "stooging" for car owner Carl Oliver and drivers such as Bud

Camden and Jimmy Reece. By 1953, when he met Jack Zink, Dennie was already part of the racecar culture of Oklahoma City and Tulsa.[39]

At the time, Jack was keeping the stock car driven by Jimmy Reece in Oklahoma City, stored at the Ford dealership on Britton Road owned by Jack's uncle, Pat Pugh. Jack, with little time between races, hired Dennie to work on it in the evenings and on weekends. Dennie subsequently built another '37 Ford for the team, then joined Jack in an experiment of building a '38 Chevrolet to challenge the long dominant Fords. They reworked the chassis of what one reporter called a "bedraggled" old car, installed a GMC truck engine, and started fine tuning the suspension until it was race ready.

Jack, racing under the name of Bob Jones, drove the car. When it hit the tracks in 1954 the Chevy was dominant, "the terror of the Tulsa and Oklahoma City ovals" as one sports writer wrote. On two occasions in Oklahoma City, Jack sped the car to triumph in three races on a single card, blowing away "the Fords, the late model Oldsmobiles, Buicks, and assorted other racing machinery." Dennie Moore, the architect of the car, had found a home on the Zink Racing Team.[40]

Stockcar racing was just what Jack needed from 1950 to 1954 as he started his business career. He could be in New Jersey or Los Angeles working on a burner installation for a day or a week, fly back to Oklahoma, and find a stockcar race going on somewhere in the state every night of the week. With little advance preparation, he could load the car, get to a nearby track, and satisfy his need for speed and competition.

There was much to enjoy in the new sport. He thrived on the camaraderie with people like Jimmy Reece, Felix Graves, Cecil Green, and Dennie Moore. He liked the speed and the thrill of victory. But even with the public recognition of his ability as both a car owner and as a driver, there was something missing that Jack needed. It was the pursuit of being the best, the fastest, and the winner at the highest level. And in racing, that meant one thing, the Indianapolis 500, the greatest test of cars and driving skills in the world.

For Jack, Indy was the next challenge.

By 1952 the John Zink Racing Team (facing page) had both a short wheel-base Midget car (left) and the full size Indianapolis-style race car that did well in the Championship Series with Jimmy Reece behind the wheel.

To Finish First, First You Must Finish

"The six key words to success are never, never, never, never give up."

Jack Zink

CHAPTER THREE

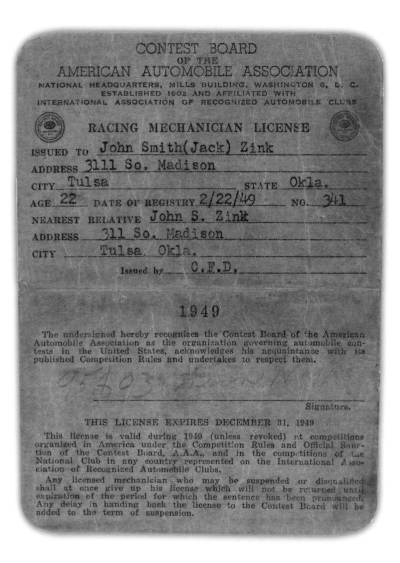

In 1949 Jack received his first certification as a racing mechanic from the American Automobile Association. Six years later (page 52), Jack posed with his winning team at the Indianapolis 500. With Jack are driver Bob Sweikert (in the car) and A.J. Watson (next to Jack).

In 1950 there was one track, one race that defined the ultimate glory in the world of automobile racing. The track was the Indianapolis Motor Speedway and the race was the 500-mile classic held every Memorial Day.

The track had been built in 1909 on the northwest edge of Indianapolis, Indiana, the center of automobile research and development in the United States at that time. The rectangular shaped track was two and a half miles long, fifty feet wide in the straight-aways, sixty feet wide in the turns, with the front and back stretches 3,300 feet long and the north and south stretches 660 feet long. The four turns, banked at sixteen degrees, were 1,320 feet long. Like every other track in the country, the surface was originally dirt, but after a series of crashes, the owners added a layer of 3.2 million grouted bricks to make it the fastest, safest track in the world. The first 500-mile classic was staged on May 30, 1911, won by Ray Harroun at an average speed of 74.59 miles per hour.

The Speedway, like the cars and the 500-mile classic, evolved through the years. The brick surface ate tires and cars as speeds increased, so the ownership group led by World War I flying ace Eddy Rickenbacker covered the track with asphalt in 1935. The original wooden grandstands, which held 100,000 spectators, were gradually replaced with steel and concrete structures. New roads, overhead bridges for pedestrian traffic, and new entrances were added to accommodate another 100,000 spectators in the infield and parking for 25,000 automobiles. By 1949, when Bill Holland won the race with an average speed of 121.327 mph, the Indianapolis 500 was world famous as the ultimate test of cars and drivers. [1]

Several Oklahomans succumbed to the allure of the Indianapolis 500. In 1946, when the races resumed after the war, Tulsa used car dealer, Ervin Wolfe, purchased a Shaw chassis, installed the latest 271-cubic-inch, four-cylinder Offenhauser, and finished eighth in his inaugural run with Frank Wearne at the wheel. The next year, with Paul Russo driving, the same car qualified for the seventh row, but wrecked on the twenty-fourth lap. After failing to qualify in 1948, Wolfe returned to the classic in 1949 with a new Kurtis-Kraft 2000 chassis powered by the newest, hottest Offenhauser and finished fifth with Joie Chitwood driving. [2]

Another Oklahoman who could not resist the lure of Indy was M.A. Walker of Oklahoma City. Walker, born in Gotebo, Oklahoma, in 1910, was raised on a farm until drought and the Great Depression sent him looking for new opportunities. He attended electrician's school and found a job wiring catalog houses sold by Montgomery Ward. By the end of World War II he had his own electrical contracting firm.

In 1949 Walker went to the midget car races at Taft Stadium in Oklahoma City and was instantly hooked. He bought a Kurtis-Kraft midget, ran it on the Southwest circuit, and eventually became a Kurtis-Kraft dealer selling parts to the rapidly expanding circle of racecar owners. Within the year he was determined to go to the next level of racing, the Indianapolis 500 and the Championship Trail.

Walker consulted with his friend and local racing enthusiast, Bill Jones of Oklahoma City. Jones, a native of Jennings, Oklahoma, was the owner of a local plating and speed shop and had been around boat racing since the mid-1930s and midget car racing since 1946, when he built his own car. He knew Walker and just about everybody else in the local racing world. Walker told him he wanted to sell his midget car and buy the most recent Kurtis-Kraft Indy-style car. Would he help? Walker went to California and purchased a Kurtis-Kraft 3000, one of only four produced that year with a fuel-injected, 270-cubic inch Offy. He also bought a Burbank trailer and enlisted one of the racing world's best known engine experts, Takio "Chickie" Hirashima, to be the team's chief mechanic. Bill Jones was asked to be on the team, and together, they recruited local racing hero and Houston native, Cecil Green, to be the driver. All they needed was the financial backing of a sponsor to help cover the cost of tires and a month of practice and qualifying at Indy. For that, they looked northeast up Route 66 to Tulsa and one of the region's hottest racing tandems, John and Jack Zink. [3]

Jack was more than just a team owner. He was a mechanic, the pit crew chief, and a devoted fan of car racing.

Jack, with his youthful enthusiasm for racing, was immediately taken with the idea of going to the Indianapolis 500. He had been a team leader, chief mechanic, and driver for a successful team that had won at the local, state, and regional levels in both midgets and stock cars. Full of self-confidence, he was ready for the big leagues.

His father, John, was also ready to move up. Although he did not manage the racing team, he was interested as both an active spectator

Jack had worked on cars since he was a teenager. His first design was a simple engine mounted on two boards with no clutch. To accelerate, he leaned one direction, tightening a drive belt. To slow down, he leaned the other way, loosening the belt.

and as a proud father. Moreover, the racing team was doing well, winning races, titles, and enough money to justify the mounting expenses. There also was the marketing potential of team sponsorship.

Racing was becoming big business, attracting hundreds of thousands of fans who knew the drivers, recognized the cars, and remembered the sponsors' names. John, as a creative businessman, knew that he needed greater name recognition in two markets. One was the industrial sector, anywhere burners were needed, which was increasingly becoming international with new markets opening overseas. World famous events, such as the Indy 500, might open doors to new customers. Then there was the mass consumer market for floor furnaces, evaporative coolers, attic fans, and more recently, innovative central heating units developed by the John Zink Company to satisfy the booming residential housing market. When M.A. Walker asked him to sponsor his Indy car in 1950, John knew that millions of potential customers would be watching in person, listening on the radio, and reading about the race in the newspapers. He said yes.

On the way to Indy, the inaugural John Zink Special took a short detour to Texas, where Clark Gable's new racing movie "To Please a Lady" was being shot. The production crew wanted to use Walker's beautiful new, powder blue Kurtis-Kraft as the featured racecar. Bill Jones hauled the car to Arlington, worked with technical advisor Johnny Parsons for the shots, and then took off for the race about three weeks later.[4]

With Chickie calling the shots and Bill Jones, M.A. Walker, and Jack in the pits, the crew started preparing the car for qualifying. Meanwhile, Indy veteran Tony Bettenhausen took the rookie driver, Cecil Green, under his wing and showed him how to run the unique turns of Indy. On May 20, more than a week before the race, Green pushed the John Zink Special to the third fastest qualifying speed in Indy history, an average speed of 132.910 over the ten-mile trip. On race day, May 30, 1950, an optimistic John Zink was in the grandstand with a large party of Tulsans when the race began. [5]

The new Kurtis-Kraft ran well, with a lower center of gravity and the powerful Offy keeping Green among the frontrunners and avoiding wrecks. Almost three hours later, as the leaders approached the 137th lap, a gentle rain started and the cars began to slide. When the yellow flag came out, most of the drivers pulled into the pits for new tires and more fuel, but Chickie looked at the skies and guessed that heavy rains were on the way. He turned to Bill Jones, who was manning the chalkboard, and told him to change the message from "Pit stop" to "Don't stop, it's about to rain." When the rains hit and the race was called, Green had the John Zink Special in fourth place, a great finish for a rookie driver with a new team.[6]

With newfound respect and the $10,963 purse for their fourth-place finish at Indy, the John Zink Special team set off to conquer the Championship Trail, a fourteen-stop circuit of open-wheeled, dirt-track racing that stretched from Sacramento on the west to Syracuse on the east. Although the car did not win any of the races, Green consistently finished in the money, placing third in Detroit, fifth in Springfield, sixth in Phoenix, and fourth in Darlington (South Carolina). When the season came to an end, the John Zink Special stood fourth in the nation. [7]

Both Jack and John Zink were pleased with their first year on the Indy circuit. Jack, already a master mechanic with a knack for innovation, learned more about the teamwork, the strategies, and the qualities of drivers needed for the test at Indy. John, who wanted the company name splashed across the country, got that plus a great time hosting his co-workers and friends as a team sponsor at the world's largest, most prestigious sporting event. They both agreed—they would stay with the Walker team another season.

The 1951 campaign for the John Zink Special began with the same car, the same engine, and the same team, but with a different color paint scheme, yellow with white lettering. Cecil was behind the wheel again, with Bill Jones and Jack joining Walker in the pits. For the second time, they qualified on the fourth row and ran well early in the race, even leading for a few laps. Then the casualties started falling. By the mid-way point of the race, half of the field was out, and at lap eighty a connecting rod broke on the well-worn Offy pushing the Zink car. Only nine cars out of thirty-three finished the Indy classic that year. [8]

Following Indy, the John Zink Special started well on the Championship Trail, coming in second at Milwaukee, third at Langhorne, Pennsylvania, and third at Darlington before the engine showed strains of constant use. Unable to afford a new engine, Jones took the car back to Oklahoma City to rebuild the engine. Cecil Green, temporarily without a ride, took the wheel driving for Clay Smith. Tragically, he was involved in a wreck

Jack and Jimmy Reece prepared for the physically demanding Championship Series and its first stop, the Indianapolis Speedway.

Jimmy Reece was a mechanic who had grown up around his driver/mechanic father, a Cushman motorcycle dealer in Oklahoma City.

The John Zink racing team overcame a series of mechanical problems during qualifying for the 1952 Indianapolis 500. Here, with M.A. Walker (left) looking on, Jack and Jimmy pulled the Offenhauser from the chassis.

Jimmy Reece with "John's Big Box" in front of the team's garage at the Indianapolis Speedway.

and killed. The rest of the season the team juggled drivers, first with Troy Ruttman, then with a rising star on the national scene, Bill Vukovich, and finally with Joe James, who between them drove the aging car to six top ten finishes by the end of the season. [9]

Success on the Championship Trail, even if it was as a team sponsor, bolstered Jack's confidence as a racecar team leader. His midgets had been competitive for five years, with city, state, and regional championships, followed by three years of success with stockcars both as an owner and a driver, and involvement as an Indy team sponsor. He also was doing well in his new job, representing his father across the country and working with the research team at the John Zink Company to develop new industrial products and processes that would carry the company to international prominence within the decade. Still single, still ambitious, Jack at the age of twenty-four was once again ready for a new challenge.

Jack talked to his father. If they were going to sponsor a car at Indy, which demanded both time and money, why not own the car? After all, the Walker car had earned enough prize money the first year to offset most of the expenses and pay for part of the car. And if they were going back to Indy, why not have the best equipment and control over the team? John, a practical businessman as well as a noted sportsman, agreed. They would go back to the Indianapolis 500 in 1952, but they would go as sponsor, owner, and team leader.

Jack called his friend Bill Jones, a racing veteran who had spent the previous two years managing the Walker car on the road, and asked him to put together a budget. What would it take to field a team not just to compete, not just to qualify, but to win the race? He also wanted Bill to be on the pit crew. Jimmy Reece, the twenty-two year-old midget car driver and stockcar driver for Jack the previous two seasons, would be at the wheel.[10]

As veterans at Indy knew, there were three types of team owners. Some were under-financed with second tier cars hoping to get lucky. Others were well financed with good cars but content to compete without expecting to win. Then there was the third kind of owner who was well financed, wanted the best equipment and best drivers, and whose only goal was to win. John and Jack Zink were in the last category. Once again,

Cecil Green, one of the many drivers Jack recruited and supported throughout his career. Jack was proud that no one was ever killed while driving for him.

Jack (left) talking with Jimmy Reece as they prepared for the 1952 edition of the Indianapolis 500. It was in this car that Jimmy installed the "Jesus bar."

they started that quest by going to the most successful chassis designer in the world, Frank Kurtis.

Kurtis was already a legend, ranking second in Indy lore only to Harry Miller, whose cars had sat on the pole eleven times, won six races, and held all three positions in the front row five times. (The fastest car during qualifying events "sits on the pole," or starts on the inside of the track at the pole, essentially at the front of the pack.) In his heyday from 1946 to 1956, Kurtis had eight cars sit on the pole with five wins and four front rows. Unlike Miller, who was a genius in engine technology, Kurtis was a chassis man who pioneered innovations such as aviation-type tube framing, torsion bar suspension, off-set weight distribution, and stream-lined bodies that cut through the air and reduced drag. His designs were matched by the quality of the era's dominant engine, the four-cylinder Offenhauser. In thirty-seven attempts, from 1935 to 1976, Offenhauser engines won Indy twenty-nine times. In 1952, if you wanted to win at the Indianapolis 500, you ran a Kurtis-Kraft powered by an Offenhauser. [11]

Jack bought the most recent version of the Kurtis-Kraft Championship car, a KK-4000, which was the last of the Kurtis cars designed for both the pavement of Indianapolis and the dirt tracks on the rest of the schedule. It was a traditional upright car, designed to "get a bite" on the dirt tracks, with conventional solid axles suspended with parallel torsion bars contained in tubes. The 270-cubic-inch Offy produced 360-horse power at 5,000 rpm. The total package cost approximately $20,000 (about $160,000 in 2008 dollars). [12]

A month before Indy, Jack and Jimmy Reece finished a Saturday evening stockcar race in Oklahoma City and immediately set out for Indianapolis in a pickup truck loaded with tools and pulling a trailer with the new car, painted black with orange letters and the number 37. They arrived at the Speedway on Sunday, late in the day. When they pulled up to the gate, the grizzled registrar, Frankie Bain, took one look at the two young men and asked them who they were. Jack said he was the car

Jack posed for this photograph on the short stretch of bricks at the Indianapolis Speedway. Most of the track was paved with asphalt in the 1930s, as seen in this turn with the pace car in front (pages 62 and 63).

One of the early John Zink Specials (facing page) posed for photographs with the famous Indianapolis Speedway pagoda as a backdrop.

Bob Sweikert
Driver

A.J. Watson
Mechanic

John Zink

owner and the young man with him was the driver. Bain asked how old they were. Jack answered he was twenty-four and Jimmy was twenty-two. Then the registrar asked where their mechanic was. Jack said they did not need a mechanic because they had "the perfect car." Bain then asked where they had raced. Jack said they had run '37 Ford stockcars the night before.

As Jack later remembered, Bain proceeded to lecture the young men on how "racing is a pyramid, and how Indianapolis is way up here, and you aren't even down here yet." It was a rite of passage, a hazing. When he decided he had gone on long enough, he invited the two in for a drink. When Jack said he did not drink, Bain "almost choked and said… kid, now I know you're in the wrong place." But the boys were on the grounds of the Speedway, with the best car money could buy, and they were ready to race. [13]

With a month to the race, Jack and Jimmy thought they had plenty of time to get ready. The first goal was getting Jimmy qualified to race at Indy. He had been raised around tracks, the son of G.M. Reece, a successful big car driver from 1920 to 1932, and he had won the Texas Midget championship title in 1950 and again in 1951, but he had never driven a big car. Despite some objections, the sanctioning body called AAA (American Automobile Association) gave him a chance. To their horror, during his first test run, bits of equipment started falling off the car. Reece was flagged and Jack worked late into the night making the repairs. The next day, as the tests resumed, the tank ruptured and a plume of fuel streamed out the back of the car. Again, Reece was ordered off the track and Jack made the repairs. So much for "the perfect car." [14]

As the last day of qualifying approached, Jimmy complained that he was moving around in the seat. He was a short man, probably no taller than five feet six inches, and the last thing a driver wanted to do was move around as he went into turns at 150 miles per hour. An additional problem was getting the car up to speeds that would qualify for the race. It turned out that Jimmy was gently tapping the brake as he went into the turns, in part to steady himself and in part to cope with the high speeds he had never before experienced. Something had to be done, so Jack invited Jimmy to what he called a "come to Jesus meeting."

Jack, A.J. Watson, and driver Bob Sweikert (facing page) before the 1955 race at Indianapolis.

The next morning Jack arrived in the garage and found Jimmy bending over the side of the car doing something in the cockpit. He was installing a metal bar on the pan below and to the left of the pedals. It was a footrest, a place for Jimmy to brace himself, and when the urge came, a place to "hit the brakes" without slowing the car. When he finished, they pushed the car out of the garage, started it, and waved Jimmy onto the track. The first lap he went two miles an hour faster than the previous day. Then he picked up another mile per hour, and another. As Jack recalled years later, "picking up four miles per hour in three laps at Indy was like adding an inch to your nose." When Bill Vukovich came to the pits and asked how much nitro they had added to the fuel, Jimmy told him he had put "a speed secret in the cockpit…a Jesus bar. When I go into a turn, I push my left foot on that bar and pray to Jesus I come out the other side." Jimmy "came out the other side" well enough to qualify on the eighth row. [15]

Starting ahead of the John Zink Special on race day were several innovative cars, including a newly developed, 405-cubic inch, turbocharged Cummins six-cylinder diesel, a front-wheel drive Novi eight-cylinder car, and a V-12 Ferrari, driven by Italian Grand Prix champion Alberto Ascari. Despite their faster qualifying speeds, Jimmy kept up with them early in the race and saw each fall out with mechanical problems. His own car purred along beautifully, never missing a beat. Even the first pit stop went well, getting the car back on the track in less than sixty seconds. Then came the second pit at the 300-mile mark, which did not go as well. Due to a fuel bladder than had been added to the faulty fuel tank, a constricted flow of fuel caused the engine to stall. It took Jack and the pit team more than a full minute to get the tires changed, the fuel in, and the engine started, valuable time that cost them more than half a lap. At the finish Jimmy took the checkered flag in seventh place, less than a lap behind the winning car driven by Troy Ruttman. [16]

"Jimmy drove a marvelous race and certainly lived up to what we knew he could do," Jack told the press after the race. "This was our first year in the big race and we were feeling our way along. Next year we should be a lot wiser." Jack was pleased with the seventh place finish and the $6,368 purse that came with it, but he was not yet satisfied because he knew they could work harder and improve even more. [17]

The learning curve continued on the Championship Trail, with Jack as chief mechanic keeping the car in great condition and Jimmy proving he was a master on the dirt tracks as well. At Milwaukee they came in fifth, followed by eighth place finishes at Springfield and again at Milwaukee. Then came a string of finishes from tenth to fifteenth place, but in the money. By the end of the campaign, the team had qualified for every race (one of only four that year to accomplish that feat), come in ninth in the national point standings, and won another $5,000 in purses, bringing the seasonal winnings to more than $11,000. For Jack, it was a good showing for a young team; for John, it was a good return on his investment. [18]

Over the winter, Jack decided he could not juggle the rigors of his increasingly demanding business career and his role as chief mechanic for the team. One or the other had to go, and business came first, so he lured long time Indy veteran car owner, Ervin Wolfe, to lead the coming campaign. With the occasional help of Jack and the full time assistance of Tulsa mechanic Dave Burkett, Wolfe rebuilt the engine. They added high compression pistons, which raised the compression ratio to 15:1, compared to a ratio of 6:1 in most passenger cars. They ordered more than $10,000 in spare parts, which included sixteen new twelve-inch wide wheels and tires from Firestone that promised to add three miles per hour to any car. And with memories of the leaky fuel tank from the previous year, they added three coats of fiberglass and more sturdy straps to the sixty-gallon aluminum tank. By May 1, 1953, they had the car reassembled and ready for the trip to Indy. [19]

Jimmy Reece, who had been on leave from the Air Force for the previous year's race, could not get loose for a return run at Indy. At the wheel of the turquoise car with orange letters was Jerry Hoyt, a twenty-four year-old native of Indianapolis who had started driving midget racecars at the age of twelve. He had been at the wheel in two Indy 500s, but never finished. His instructions from Wolfe and Zink were simple; forget about pacing the car and go as fast and as far as you can. As Wolfe said to the press, "Mr. Zink wants a winner." [20]

Hoyt qualified the car for the third row with a speed of 135.731, well behind the clear favorite, Bill Vukovich, who led all qualifiers with a speed of 138.392. Vuky, known as the "Mad Russian," was driving the first true roadster from Kurtis designed specifically for Indy. The outstanding innovation that gave him an advantage and defined the "roadster" was

an engine tilted at an angle, which ran the drive shaft down the left side of the car, allowed the driver to sit directly on the pan about four inches above the pavement, and pushed the center weight of the car to the inside. The lower profile reduced drag, while the left side weight bias helped the driver hug the curves at faster speeds. [21]

When the race began, the air temperature was ninety degrees, but the track temperature was 130 degrees. Hoyt had a good start, avoiding wrecks on the third, fifty-third, and seventy-sixth laps, but he and many of the drivers could not handle the heat. One driver, Carl Scarborough, came into the pits on the seventieth lap and collapsed. He was taken to the hospital where he died from heat exhaustion. Then on lap 107, with Hoyt in seventh place, he went into a deliberate spin to avoid a wreck. He came into the pits, almost unconscious, and was told he could not continue due to the suffocating heat. At the end of the race only ten cars were still on the track. [22]

The Championship Trail campaign, without Jack as the team leader, did not get much better, even with a third place finish at Milwaukee that earned a $2,266 purse. Thereafter, the car suffered back luck. At Springfield, Hoyt worked his way from the back row to third place when a wheel broke and sent the car plunging into the wall on lap seventy-six. Two weeks later, at Milwaukee, he was in second place at lap 101 when a tire blew out, hurtling the car into the wall and flipping it end over end. Hoyt was not injured but the car was badly damaged; it did not start another race that year. [23]

In 1954 Jack hired Ervin Wolfe's chief assistant, Dave Burkett, as the new full time chief mechanic to take care of the KK-4000 in its third year. Painted red with white letters, the hybrid car underwent several modifications. They replaced the torsion bar suspension with more traditional springs, added a ramjet to direct air into the fuel injectors, and rebuilt the engine once again. They also changed drivers, hiring Gene Hartley, a twenty-eight-year-old veteran from Roanoke, Indiana, who had run at Indy several times, although never finishing higher than sixteenth place. At qualifying, with the much-traveled Jack back on the team making constant changes to the chassis, Hartley got the speed up to 139.061, the fastest the car had ever gone and good enough for a spot on the sixth row. [24]

For the second year in a row Bill Vukovich took the first place checkered flag in his Kurtis-Kraft 500A. Hartley, running well in the early going, was moving up on the field until lap 168 when the clutch went out. The John Zink Special finished twenty-third, good for a purse of $2,814. The rest of the season did not get much better, with sixth and seventh place finishes at the two races in Milwaukee, a seventh place finish in Phoenix, and a twelfth place finish in Du Quoin, Illinois. At the other venues, the car was either too slow to qualify or was not entered. For both Jack and John, this was not good enough. They wanted a change. [25]

A fter three years of racing at Indy, Jack knew what he had to do to have a chance at winning the big race in 1955. To the press, he said he needed good luck, but the engineer in him knew better. Winning at Indy took teamwork, a fast car, a great driver, and a good support team led by a great chief mechanic. And then a little luck as well.

The first task was pulling together the right team, and for that, he needed a chief mechanic who knew racecars inside and out, especially the kind that could go 140 miles per hour for 500 miles. The best place to find such a man was at Indy, and Jack had watched the various team leaders, not only for their results on the track, but also for their personalities. Did he get along well with team owners and drivers? Was he open to innovations and the sharing of knowledge? Could he keep his ego in check and focus on winning? Jack, as he moved through the small world of Indy each May, saw one man who fit that profile. It was A.J. Watson.

Abram Joe Watson, better known as A.J., grew up in Ohio, joined the Army Air Corps during World War II, and served as a navigator on B-17s. At war's end, he moved to Southern California to attend college and work in his father's dolly manufacturing shop. One day in late 1946, a group of young men came to the shop to have a trailer built for their car, a combination street rod and racer known as a "track roadster." A.J. attended a race and was immediately hooked. He built his own car, intending to be the driver, but after a few laps claimed he had stomach trouble. "I had no guts," he said. [26]

Bob Sweikert (right) posed before the 1955 Indianapolis 500 with the world's number one ranked driver, Bill Vukovich, who had won the race in 1953 and 1954.

He sold his first hotrod, then built and sold three more. The sport grew rapidly in Southern California, with an association to sanction races by 1947 and a growing circle of young owner/drivers who included Troy Ruttman, Pat Flaherty, Jim Rathmann, Dick Rathmann, Jack McGrath, and Manuel Ayulo. Many of them would go on to race at Indy, and by 1949 A.J. had built a big car for the 500. With Pat Flaherty as his driver, they went to Indy but failed to qualify. The next year he was back with a different car, affectionately known as the "Pots and Pans Special," and started the race on the sixth row with Dick Rathmann driving. The drive shaft broke on the twenty-fifth lap. [27]

Without the money to keep the car on the Championship Trail, A.J. sold it to Southern California Lincoln-Mercury dealer, Bob Estes, who had been running cars at Indy for several years. From 1951 to 1954 A.J. served as a mechanic on the Estes team, at first with his own chassis powered by a 270-cubic inch Offy, and then for one year running a Phillips chassis with an Offy. In those four years, with limited resources, the A.J. Watson-led team made steady progress, finishing thirty-third in 1951 (broken drive shaft), twelfth in 1952, twenty-seventh in 1953 (wreck on lap seventy-six), and seventh in 1954. That winter, back at his home in Southern California, A.J. received a phone call from his friend, Jack Zink, of Tulsa, Oklahoma. The full time businessman, part time race team owner wanted A.J. to be his chief mechanic, and to get him, he would double his salary from $75 a week to $150 a week. A.J., recently married with plans to start a family, accepted the offer. [28]

With a chief mechanic, Jack needed a new car. The old KK-4000 purchased in 1952 had been designed as a hybrid, part dirt car with a "bite," part paved-track car that could power through the turns at Indy. It might still win on the Championship Trail, but it was clear to Jack that if he wanted to win at Indy, he had to have one of the cars that had won two years in a row, a Kurtis Kraft 500, designed specifically for the paved surface at the Speedway. He talked to his father and explained that it could cost as much as $32,000 to field a team: $20,000 for the car, $10,000 in expenses, and $2,000 for tires (an investment totaling roughly a quarter of a million in 2008 dollars). John quickly agreed. If they were going back

The start of the 1955 Indianapolis 500 (facing page). The John Zink Special started the race in the middle of the fifth row after making the field with a qualifying speed of 139.996 miles per hour.

to Indy, they needed whatever it took to win. They would buy a new car. [29]

Jack and A.J. went to Frank Kurtis and ordered a slightly altered version of the first true roadster that had been dominant since 1952. Designated a KK-500D, it had the familiar engine setup nine inches to the left, inclined thirty-six degrees to the right, which shifted about fifty pounds of static weight to the left side and counteracted the centrifugal force in the turns at Indy. It had an aluminum body, a wheelbase of 100 inches, weighed 1,700 pounds, and had three inches of clearance and a thirty-eight-inch height to the top of the headrest. It carried sixty-five gallons of fuel, eight gallons of oil for the engine, and four gallons of water in the radiator. When A.J. picked it up at the factory, the car was unfinished, ready to be tailor made for the driver. [30]

For several years Jack had been watching a young driver from Southern California named Bob Sweikert. Like Jack, Sweikert had been drawn to cars as a teenager. To the surprise of his parents, he "souped up" a Model A Ford to do 115 miles per hour. After serving in World War II, he opened an auto repair shop but kept working on hot rods, then started racing them. In 1947, when his family told him to make a choice between racing and the business, he chose the former. The next year he won the California Roadster Championship title, then won the California Indoor Midget Championship and the Pacific Coast Big Car Championship in 1949. He even qualified for Indy in 1950. He set several sprint car records across the country and improved his performances at Indy from a twenty-sixth place finish in 1952, to a twentieth place finish in 1953, and a fourteenth place finish in 1954. As a bonus, he was a great mechanic and Jack liked him. Considering that Sweikert and A.J. had been good friends since the Southern California roadster racing days of the late 1940s, it seemed like a match made in heaven. [31]

With a car, a driver, and a chief mechanic, Jack assembled the rest of his team. For the pit crew, he hired Bob DeBisschop of Walnut Creek, California, a young man in his early twenties who had worked on the KK-500D in the Kurtis shops. As an Offenhauser specialist, he complemented A.J., whose specialty was chassis work. Then he hired Henry and Bob Meyers, brothers from Dayton, Ohio, who were Indy veterans and had been on the Andy Linden pit crew in 1954 when their team took only twenty-nine seconds for a full pit stop. Others hired for the race were veterans

TO INDY AND BEYOND: THE LIFE OF RACING LEGEND JACK ZINK

Willie Wilk of Grand Rapids, Michigan, and Larry Shinoda of Los Angeles. [32]

As Jack knew, a good pit crew could make the difference between winning and just finishing. In a race, every car had to make at least two pit stops, taking an average of sixty seconds per stop. If a team could cut only ten seconds from each pit stop, it would save a mile on the track. If the stops were trimmed by twenty seconds, it was a two-mile advantage. Then there was the communication between the pit crew and the driver. There were no two-way radios in use at the time, so the only way to talk was sign language, either through physical gestures or written on a blackboard and flashed at the driver as he screamed by. To get an advantage in pit stops and team communication, Jack drilled the crew in the weeks leading to the race.

First came the race language, which was familiar to all the veterans. What was their position in the race? How many laps remained? How far ahead was he? Should he push the car or save the tires? Some members of the crew had to watch the tires through binoculars to monitor tire tread. Others had to keep lap times and watch for lagging. One person barked directions while another wrote messages on the chalkboard and made sure the driver understood. When the car entered the pits, four members of the team jumped the fence and changed tires, added fuel, and talked to the driver. Occasionally, after wrecks, the crew might straighten or cut away a part of the body. Because every second counted, they had to be prepared for every possibility.

The preparation included a strategy for the race. Jack knew that at least twenty-five of the thirty-three cars were capable of winning, including the car driven by two-time winner, Bill Vukovich. Of the starting cars, twenty were Kurtis-Krafts with engines identical to one powering the John Zink Special. The strategy was to pass the slower cars as early as possible, then lay back while hard charging Vukovich battled his top challenger, Jack McGrath. The Zink team calculated that to finish in the top five, they would have to average at least 135 miles per hour, and to win they would have to avoid wrecks, get the car as ready as it could be, and execute during every pit stop. [33]

Although Jack was heard to say many times, "to finish first, first you must finish," the 1955 Indy team found it equally important that "to fin-

Jack (left with a hat) ran the pit crew, which included signaling drivers during the race on tire conditions, fuel status, and race strategies.

ish first, first you must start." On the first two qualifying attempts, the car was flagged off the track for running too slow. Something was wrong. Then, on a practice run, the engine seized and broke the block. Another engine was hastily secured, but Jack, A.J., and Sweikert had to break it down and go through every part as the last day of qualifying approached. Before it was reassembled, A.J. got a distressing call from Los Angeles; his wife had been rushed to the hospital and she was having a difficult delivery of their first child. A.J., with Jack's blessing, rushed to the airport and caught a plane for home. With the car in what he called "a thousand pieces," A.J. left a note behind for Sweikert that read: "Have the crew put the chassis together. You build the engine." Sweikert, with Jack's help, built the engine, mounted it in the reassembled car, and pushed it out of the garage for their last attempt at making the field of thirty-three. This time the car ran well and Sweikert drove it to an average speed of 139.996, the fourteenth fastest time and good for a spot in the middle of the fifth row. Another piece of good news was the return of A.J. to the team following the birth of his child. [34]

Jack's father, John, was making his own preparations for the race. He invited forty-one Tulsans to go with him to the Speedway, including thirty employees from the John Zink Company, which was footing the bills. They chartered a bus, packed it with a tent and supplies, and drove to Indianapolis a week before the big race. The transplanted Tulsa village, which included a truck trailer converted to a dormitory, was set up near the track amid the swirling carnival that had become a pre-race ritual. Within a block were bingo tents, shooting galleries, a "shouting" church revival, a midget car racetrack, and what one reporter called "pitchmen of every description." On race day, John proudly led his entourage to the grandstands to watch the race. [35]

An hour before the race began, *Tulsa Tribune* reporter Ed Spilman joined Jack, A.J., and Sweikert in the garage. There was an uneasy tension with little being said. For days, the running joke around the team had been Sweikert's dream of building a new house on a wooded acreage on the outskirts of Indianapolis. He talked about it when they were working on the engine. He talked about it when they were eating lunch. With the race about to start, he broke the uneasy silence: "In about four hours I'm going to be able to make the down payment on that house." Smiles all around broke the tension as they began to push the car toward the track.[36]

For the first time, Speedway owner Tony Hulman had the honor of shouting, "Gentlemen, start your engines." With a roar filling the air, the cars followed the official pace car, a 1955 Chevrolet "Turbo-Fire" Bel Air, for one lap and then charged ahead under the green flag. Jack McGrath, driving a KK-500C, took the lead for the first three laps, but was passed by Bill Vukovich, who had moved up from his fifth-place starting position. Sweikert, following the pre-race plan, hung back and stayed out of trouble. The thrilling fight for the lead lasted until lap fifty-seven, when the axle on Rodger Ward's car shattered, sending him into the wall. As cars scrambled to avoid Ward, two cars got tangled, started spinning, and hit the rear of Vukovich's car. Out of control, the champion's car flew into the air, end over end, and landed upside down outside the track. Vukovich was killed instantly. [37]

With a yellow flag to clear the track, Sweikert pulled into the pits for his first stop. The crew, which had gone through numerous drills the previous two days, went into action when trouble hit. With all four tires off, the back jack failed and the car hit the pavement, landing on the disk brakes. The crew scrambled to get the car jacked up again, put new tires on, and topped off the fuel tank. Hoping that the fall had not done any damage, Sweikert roared back onto the track. Even with the accident, the pit stop had taken only sixty-five seconds. [38]

Under a green flag, the race resumed with defending national champion, Jimmy Bryan, leading the next thirty-one laps before Sweikert pressed him and then passed him on lap eighty-nine to take the lead. The John Zink Special held the lead at the mid-way point in the race, with Art Cross in second place and Johnnie Parsons in third. At the 300-mile mark, Sweikert had a minute lead on Cross, when he was signaled to come in for his second pit stop. Again, Jack's crew flew into action, and this time, with the outcome of the race in the balance, it went flawlessly. In only twenty-six seconds, the crew changed the tires, fueled the car, and got it back on the track in third place. [39]

Within minutes, the two leaders also pitted and Sweikert roared into the lead once again, averaging between 132 and 137 miles per hour depending on the pressure from the challengers. Meanwhile, a car driven by Tulsa-native Tony Bettenshausen and owned by the Chapman family

of Tulsa was making a move toward the lead pack. Tony moved into third after a duel with Freeland, then began battling Cross for second. On the 192nd lap, only eight laps from the end, the Zink team was told by track officials that the Chapman car was only fifteen seconds behind Sweikert. Then the team went into crisis mode again.

According to his calculations, Jack was not sure that his car had enough fuel to finish. The worst-case scenario had the fuel giving out on lap 195, while the best-case scenario had them finishing with less than a gallon to spare. With Bettenhausen closing in, they could neither afford another pit stop nor allow Sweikert to slow down to conserve fuel. They had to take a chance and wave him on to a mad dash to the checkered flag. Those last five laps, as the crew held their collective breath, Sweikert kept roaring by, one agonizing lap at a time. Four laps to go. Three laps to go. Two laps to go. One lap. Then, the checkered flag...and pandemonium. The John Zink team had won the 1955 Indianapolis 500. [40]

As his winning car sped by, Jack leaped into the air and screamed to his team members, "We're finally taking that big cup to Tulsa." He was referring to the Borg-Warner Trophy, a five-foot tall gleaming mass of silver that included the name of every winning car and driver dating to 1911. In the world of car racing, there was no greater prize. [41]

After taking the winner's lap, Sweikert pulled into victory lane with the crowds still screaming and the photographers converging into an impenetrable wall around the car. Dinah Shore, the celebrity guest for the race, greeted the winning driver with a kiss. One photographer captured the joy of the moment as Jack stood on the back of the car, the Borg-Warner Trophy under his right arm, as he looked into the crowd for his father so he could join them in the winner's circle.

"Oh, brother, what a thrill," Jack said to the gang of reporters. "I'm so glad I can hardly talk." He hugged his driver. "Sweikert drove a marvelous race," Jack said. "He's a big, strong fellow with excellent driving ability. We knew he was ready for this one." Jack also heaped praise on his chief mechanic, A.J. Watson, a man of few words. A.J. modestly gave credit to the team, with special praise for Sweikert. "This man is the best racing mechanic in the whole world," he said to the crowd as he threw his arms

To keep pit stops to less than sixty seconds, Jack practiced the team in the weeks leading up to race day. Here, they change tires and refuel the car.

TO INDY AND BEYOND: THE LIFE OF RACING LEGEND JACK ZINK

TO FINISH FIRST, FIRST YOU MUST FINISH

around the driver. "And you're the best blankety-blank race car driver who ever crawled into a car." Almost fifty years later, A.J. Watson would maintain that Bob Sweikert was the best driver he ever saw. "He was an A.J. Foyt before there was an A.J. Foyt," referring to the part mechanic, part driver who would dominate big time racing in the 1960s and 1970s. [42]

Even the elder Zink could not restrain himself. After the car was returned to the garage, one reporter said John was "wreathed in smiles" as he patted the team members on the back. "You've made me proud," he said, "but the racing team is my son's baby and this is his day." In a later interview with a reporter Jack returned the gratitude, "Dad was happy. You know, he's been footing the bill for six years now. He had confidence in us, for which we are awfully grateful." The Zink team—son, father, mechanic, and driver—had done well. They were the winners of the Indianapolis 500. [43]

Bob Sweikert, with the Borg-Warner Trophy, smiles after the victory that earned him more than $100,000 in winnings and endorsements.

Bob Sweikert (pages 76 and 77) was the winning driver in the 1955 Indianapolis 500. He was greeted with kisses and the Borg-Warner Trophy in Victory Lane.

Back home in Tulsa, Jack (facing page) displayed the winning car at a downtown location and let visitors get behind the wheel.

Lapping the Field

"We don't ever have any perfected products ...
we work continuously to improve them all."

Jack Zink

CHAPTER FOUR

At the age of twenty-six, Jack Zink found himself and his team members at the pinnacle of the racing world—they were the winners of the Indianapolis 500. For eight years he had been building, driving, and managing racecars, pulling close to him people who could work together to achieve a common goal. During that same time, he had finished college, joined his father's company, and established himself as an innovative engineer who could solve his clients' problems. The challenge suddenly went from getting to the top to staying on top.

Staying on top in the world of racing did not allow much time to celebrate the victory at the 1955 Indianapolis 500. For days, newspaper and television reporters peppered Jack and his team members with questions and requests for interviews, while car and parts manufacturers deluged them with requests for product endorsements and personal appearances. Firestone, which supplied the winning tires for the John Zink Special, flew Jack, chief mechanic A.J. Watson, and winning driver Bob Sweikert to New York City for a live, national appearance on the Firestone Television Hour. Back in Tulsa, the winning car was placed on display downtown where the hometown crowd joined the winning trio for yet another victory celebration. [1]

Making the win even more special was the financial windfall. The official purse for winning the Indy 500 in 1955 was $76,138, which was split between the team owner and the driver, but the unofficial net reward after personal appearances, endorsements, and special prizes was estimated to be $70,000 for the Zinks and $100,000 for Bob Sweikert. Even A.J. Watson earned additional money when the Wynn Friction Proofing Company gave him the "Winning Mechanic's Award" and a check for $1,200. A.J.'s wife told the press she would use the money to buy better furniture. Sweikert bought two new racecars and a new house. And the Zinks, after six years of investing in cars and team support at the state, regional, and national levels, balanced the books on their racing enterprise and still had money left for future investments. [2]

As if proving that this good fortune was well earned, the Zink Racing Team continued winning that year. Sweikert, shifting to the KK-4000 that Jack had purchased in 1954, hit the Championship Trail with new momentum. They finished all but two races the rest of the season, won at Syracuse, and finished no lower than fourth in all of the other races. On

September 4, 1955, several weeks before the end of the season, the John Zink Special clinched the American Automobile Association Championship, the earliest it had ever been won and the first time since 1939 that the winner of the Indy 500 had also won the Championship. Along with the additional $50,000 in winning purses came affirmation that the Zink team was the best in the world. [3]

With cash, a good team behind him, and sights set on the upcoming racing season, Jack spent what spare time he had during the winter of 1955-1956 searching for ways to go faster. As he would later say to a reporter, "We never race a car that's finished...we just quit working on it for a while so we can race." This never ending pursuit of improvement led first to an analysis of the new generation of car engines coming out of the European racing circuits. They were big, powerful, and fast. Jack consulted with his friends Carroll Shelby and Masten Gregory, two Americans who had amassed impressive records in Continental racing. Yes, they said, the big engines were fast, but they doubted that they had the stamina for the 500 miles at Indy. It would be a risk to run them, and risk was something Jack wanted to minimize. [4]

The quest for improvement even led to a quick evaluation of a new technology that had never been successfully adapted to any kind of automobile, much less an Indy-style race car that had to do 140 miles per hour. It was the turbine engine, most commonly used in aircraft. Jack had read that the Air Force was experimenting with turbines on cars, so he wrote General Curtis LeMay, commander of the Strategic Air Command (SAC), and asked for permission to inspect the car. As a racing fan, General LeMay was more than happy to meet with the winner of the Indianapolis 500. Jack traveled to SAC headquarters at Offutt Air Force Base near Omaha, Nebraska, where he met General LeMay and Major General

With one victory at Indy under his belt (page 80), Jack returned to the track with his new team that included driver, Pat Flaherty, chief mechanic, A.J. Watson, and the newest member of the team, Dennie Moore (over Jack's left shoulder).

Jack (in control room), A.J. Watson (in front of the engine), and a mechanic tested an engine at the John Zink plant garage in Tulsa.

Jack (pages 84 and 85) prepared for the 1956 Indianapolis 500 with constant pit crew drills. Here, he is using the jack to raise the car so the tires can be changed. The new car was lower and lighter than the 1955 car.

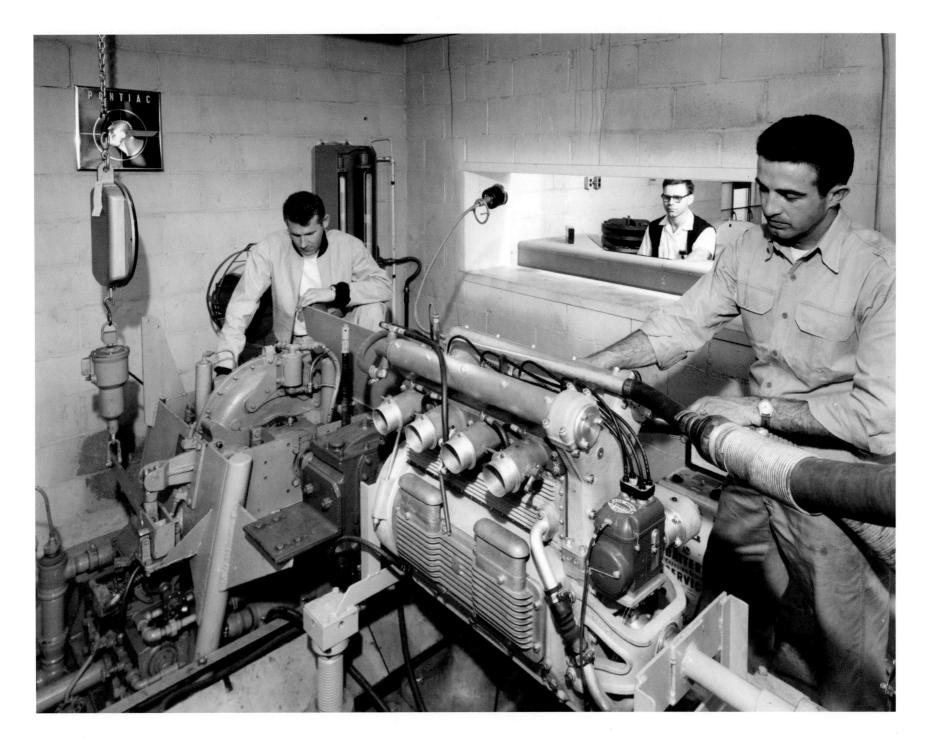

LAPPING THE FIELD

Francis Griswold, who took him immediately to the shop where their men were working on the "SAC Firebird." Jack liked what he saw. The turbine was small, lightweight, and simple, with only a few moving parts. When the commanding general asked if he wanted to test-drive it, Jack "leaped at the chance."

Jack swept up and down the runways, the turbine "whining a piercing crescendo" in the words of one reporter. Once he mastered the "peculiarities" of the car, he could tell that the engine produced tremendous torque, but he noticed that the high-end speed was not even close to what the Offenhauser could generate. He found out that the tiny engine turned out 180 horsepower, and even if that could be increased, it was a gas-guzzler. The large amount of fuel it would take to complete a 500-mile race without additional pit stops would add too much weight, even when offset by the lighter engine. The engineer in him liked the potential he saw, but the race team manager in him knew it was not the edge he was seeking. Not yet, anyway, and despite a meeting with officials from Boeing aircraft manufacturing, certainly not for the 1956 season. [5]

Instead, Jack told his chief mechanic, A.J. Watson, to "start sawing away and come up with a red hot automobile." They would run the 1955 winning car again, which would require rebuilding the engine and going through every part of the chassis, but he wanted a second car in the race that was lighter, more maneuverable, and faster. With a budget of $25,000, the thirty-year old Californian jumped at the chance to deliver what would become known as the first "Watson Roadster." [6]

Starting with the basics of the most recent Kurtis Kraft chassis, Watson looked for ways to trim weight, even if it was only an ounce or two. He reduced the diameter of the aircraft-style tubing, which cut weight, but he also wanted to make the chassis more rigid, which was essential for better handling. To compensate for the lighter material, he narrowed the entire body by four inches, but stretched it until it was five inches longer than a conventional Kurtis. To shave even more pounds, he replaced aluminum panels where he could with magnesium, a lighter material that had been considered too flammable for use on racecars. A.J. proved that it posed no safety threat.

Jack developed a special friendship with his driver, Pat Flaherty, who wore a green clover on his helmet (green was often considered an unlucky color in the world of car racing).

The new body configuration allowed him to move the rear wheels closer together until the tread from tire to tire was only forty-six-and-a-half inches. Watson theorized that the narrower tread would provide greater stability in the turns, improve tire wear, and correct what drivers called "push," the front end pulling out when power was applied through the corners. To put additional traction on the wheels, A.J. moved the front-mounted engine back toward the rear almost four inches, which in turn transferred weight from front to rear during acceleration. He replaced the old lever-type shock absorbers with two telescopic shocks on each wheel and relocated the radius rods that kept the front axle in place. Even with a larger fuel tank and new dual-system brakes, the car came in at 1,680 pounds, amazingly more than 200 pounds and ten percent lighter with a silhouette that was three inches lower than the winning car in 1955. [7]

Throughout the creative process of developing the new design, Watson consulted regularly with both Jack and John. On a trip to Tulsa in January of 1956, Watson briefed the Zinks on how his ideas would give them an edge at the Memorial Day classic. A.J., who stayed in the apartment behind the Zink house on South Madison in Tulsa, would later remember that the elder Zink once asked him to stay for dinner, even though Mrs. Zink was out of town. When he arrived in the kitchen, John pulled out a can of beans, opened the top, and put the can directly on the stovetop. They ate warm beans and talked about the car and the coming race. [8]

With a new car, a good chief mechanic, and a healthy budget to work with, Jack turned his attention to the driver for the coming Indy season. Publicly, as late as December of 1955 Jack maintained that Bob Sweikert was still his driver, but behind the scenes there was tension. After the world-famous victory at Indy in May of 1955, the winning driver had purchased two new cars with his winnings. One was a new sprint car, smaller than the Championship cars but larger than midgets, which were popular throughout the Midwest but extremely dangerous. As Jack would say years later, "the sprints killed too many good young men." The previous summer, Jerry Hoyt, driving one of Sweikert's cars in Oklahoma City, had wrecked and been killed. Still, Sweikert insisted on driving the sprints over Jack's objections. [9]

A.J. Watson was a young mechanic and race car designer from Southern California. He and Jack created one of the most dynamic teams in racing during the 1950s.

Sweikert's other new car was an Indy-style dirt car purchased from J.C. Agajanian. With Johnny Boyd at the wheel, the Sweikert car ran on the Championship circuit in 1955, competing against the Zink Special, which was still driven by Sweikert. In a sport where drivers changed teams easily and frequently, it was not surprising that these problems and conflicts ended the successful partnership between Sweikert and the Zink Racing Team. In a sad twist of fate, Bob Sweikert was killed a year later—while driving a sprint car. [10]

Jack had to find a new driver, and he had his eye on a tall, lanky, red-headed Irishman who had just won the Milwaukee 200 race on the Championship circuit. George Francis Patrick Flaherty, better known as Pat, was born in Glendale, California, in 1926. He moved to Chicago in 1949 to race in the Andy Granatelli Hurricane Hot Rod Association and made his first appearance at Indianapolis in 1949 at the wheel of A.J. Watson's first Championship car. He failed to qualify. The next year, he returned to the Speedway in one of the Granatelli cars and finished tenth. After being suspended by the AAA for a year for driving in unsanctioned races, he again drove at Indy in 1953 and 1955, finishing tenth the latter year. [11]

As one race historian put it, Flaherty was "somewhat eccentric, even by the standards of the time." He had an easygoing, almost unconcerned approach to life and racing. To friends, he said he was more interested in racing pigeons than cars, but the former did not pay as well. As if to accentuate his indifference to custom, he wore a large, green shamrock on his helmet at a time when many drivers thought green was bad luck. By 1953 he owned a tavern in Chicago called "Pat Flaherty's Lounge," where the part-time racecar driver could often be found in a starched white shirt and green bow tie serving drinks. Despite the eccentricities, he was known as a hard-charging, skilled driver who knew how to win. When Sweikert left the Zink Racing team, Jack and A.J. convinced the affable Irishman to take the wheel of their new car. [12]

Jack needed a second driver to pilot the 1955 Championship car. Initially, he offered the wheel to Sterling Moss, a young Englishman who had recently captured second place in the European World Championships

Pat Flaherty (bottom, right) posed with the other drivers in the order they qualified for the 1956 Indy 500.

Jack (second from left on facing page) put his 1955 Championship car in the 1956 race with Troy Ruttman behind the wheel.

Troy Ruttman & Crew Indianapolis Motor Speedway 1956

driving a Mercedes-Benz. Unfortunately, he was under contract to the Maserati Racing team and they would not give him a release to run at the Speedway. Jack then turned to Troy Ruttman, a talented but troubled veteran who had won the Indianapolis 500 in 1952. A native of Oklahoma who grew up in California, Troy liked the night life and gambling almost as much as racing. He fought ulcers and a series of injuries suffered during crashes, but always seemed to rebound and drive well in the big races. Rodger Ward, who saw many drivers through the years, called Ruttman "probably the most talented race driver we have ever known." In 1956 Jack and A.J., wanting an experienced driver who had proven he could win, put him in the seat of their Kurtis Kraft 500. [13]

In early May the Zink team gathered at the Speedway for practice runs and final adjustments to engines, cars, and strategies. Ruttman, known as a hard charger, was having problems getting his car up to satisfactory speeds when Jack noticed that he was going too deep into the turns before slowing. As A.J. Watson would remember almost fifty years later, Jack recommended he back off the pedal earlier and get back on the gas as he powered into the turn. It worked. By qualifying, Ruttman was running well and posted a speed of 142.484, good enough for a place on the fourth row. [14]

Flaherty had no such problems. He liked the "skinny screamer," as one reporter described Watson's new roadster. By the time for qualifying almost two weeks before the big race, he and the car were running at peak performance. Ed Spilman, a reporter with the *Tulsa Tribune*, described the record setting effort:

> The Chicago Irishman went on the track cool and detached, in contrast to the tension which hampered the efforts of some of his competitors. He lapped the big track with seemingly effortless ease. He swooped into the turns at tremendous speeds and the car hugged the asphalt surface like a leech. Down the straights, the slim stream-liner showed her top speed by clipping along at 190 mph. When the run was over, Flaherty climbed from the snug cockpit with the non-chalance of a man who has just returned from a trip to the drug store. On hand to congratulate him was the boss man of the Zink aggrega-tion, John Zink, Sr., a sportsman with varied interests.

Jack, A.J., and the rest of the team were also there to celebrate. Their in-novative roadster had just set a new qualifying record, a sizzling 145.596 miles per hour, good enough for the pole position on race day. [15]

A week before the race, Jack and friend Dick Jones returned to the Speedway driving the DeSoto "Pace Car," the symbol of their victory the year before. The cream and gold convertible was a "rolling advertisement" for Tulsa and the John Zink Company, especially when it was driven around town by the many well-known drivers who had time to spare as the teams checked and rechecked their cars. Jack used that time to run his team through pit stop practice. Joined for the first time by Dennie Moore, who had been managing Jack's stock cars for two years, the team repeat-edly jumped the fence, added sixty-five gallons of fuel to the tank, and changed all four tires. Their goal was to the complete each pit stop in less than thirty-five seconds. [16]

The team developed strategies for the two John Zink Specials. Rutt-man, driving the year-old car, would keep his speed down for the first 100 miles to conserve his tires. Flaherty, on the other hand, had no intentions of holding back. "I've got the best car and best crew," he told the press before the race. "How can I lose?" [17]

Race day dawned with rain falling, but it stopped as the crowd of more than 100,000 fans filed into the Speedway. The temperature was seventy-four degrees, with an expected high of eighty-eight before the end of the race. The wind, from the southwest, blew at fifteen miles per hour and was not a factor. The thirty-three cars were rolled out of the garages, onto the track, and lined up according to their qualifying times. Tenor Brian Sullivan sang "Back Home Again in Indiana," followed by the traditional command, "Gentlemen, start your engines." After a lap behind the pace car, the cars roared into action. [18]

On the first turn, the wary Flaherty knew he was carrying a full load of seventy-seven gallons of fuel, so he let Jim Rathmann and Pat O'Connor take the lead while he stayed on their exhaust pipes. The trio set a new first lap speed of 138.867, shaving five seconds off the previous lap record. At lap eight, a more powerful but suspect eight-cylinder Novi-Vespa driven by

The John Zink Special (right on facing page) was noticeably more aerodynamic that the other two cars on the front row for the 1956 Indianapolis 500.

A photographer caught Pat Flaherty screaming around a turn at the Indy 500 in 1956 (pages 92 and 93).

Front Row
Indianapolis Motor Speedway
= 1956 =

TO INDY AND BEYOND: THE LIFE OF RACING LEGEND JACK ZINK

Paul Russo caught up to the leaders and they signaled him to pass. O'Connor later said that Russo passed them so easily he checked his tachometer to make sure his engine had not stalled. For twenty-one laps Russo's big car ran strongly, leading the race, when a tire blew and he hit the wall on the southwest turn. The car burst into flames but Russo miraculously got out and waved to his fellow drivers. Flaherty avoided the wreck and blew into the lead. [19]

Ruttman, meanwhile, was "running like a bomb." He had moved from the fourteenth spot up to fourth and as he said later, he could have passed the cars in the third and second spots without any trouble. On the twenty-third lap, not long after Russo's spectacular wreck, he was barreling down the front straightaway at 160 miles per hour when he saw two cars about 100 yards ahead of him brush each other, lock wheels, and go into a spin. To avoid them, he dove off the track into the muddy infield, but the car hit something, leaped into the air, bounced, and came down upright in a clear area. The car was intact, but the engine had stalled and he could not get it restarted. He was out of the race. [20]

The race settled into a seesaw battle between Flaherty and O'Connor, interrupted only by five more wrecks and two pit stops while caution flags were out. Well practiced, the Zink pit crew proved again to be one of the best at Indy and got the car back on the track quickly after both pit stops, one of which took only thirty-two seconds. The effort would prove to be pivotal, as Flaherty took the lead at lap seventy-seven and never gave it up. After 500 miles of hard driving, he took the checkered flag only twenty-one seconds ahead of the second place car, the second smallest victory margin in Speedway history.[21]

After crossing the finish line, the John Zink Special inexplicably lost power, denying Flaherty his ceremonial victory lap and forcing him to coast into Victory Lane. Upon inspection, they learned that a three-eighths-of-an-inch-long metal part connecting the foot throttle to the fuel injection system had broken. If it had happened even two minutes earlier, he would have lost the race, been on the sidelines, and come in twentieth.[22]

When the winning driver emerged from the car, one reporter said

Pat Flaherty in the number 8 car (below) passes another car at speeds approaching 180 miles per hour. • Jack (left) and A.J. Watson (front right) after changing tires during a pit stop during the 1956 Indy 500 (facing page). • Pat Flaherty and the number 8 car (pages 96 and 97) took the checkered flag at the 1956 Indy 500.

TO INDY AND BEYOND: THE LIFE OF RACING LEGEND JACK ZINK

LAPPING THE FIELD

TO INDY AND BEYOND: THE LIFE OF RACING LEGEND JACK ZINK

Flaherty was "grinning like a Dublin leprechaun." His first words were, "Where's my glass of milk?" He took a big gulp and kissed his wife, took another swig, and remembered that he was supposed to get a traditional kiss from the celebrity guest, this time movie star Virginia Mayo. She wiped away some of the oily smudge on his face and gave him the kiss. He quickly turned back to his wife for another kiss. [23]

As the winning team members swarmed the winning car, each was giving credit to the others. Watson pointed to Flaherty as a great driver, while Flaherty said victory was possible only with the great team behind him. The elder John Zink, leading a Tulsa delegation of more than seventy guests who had arrived in two chartered busses, again thanked his son for putting the team together. Although pleased with the win, Jack shook his head and lamented that they had not finished one-two. Ruttman's trouble avoiding the crash already had him thinking about how to run an even better race the coming year. When pressed by a reporter for his emotions at the time, he said, "There's another race here in 365 days. We'll be back." [24]

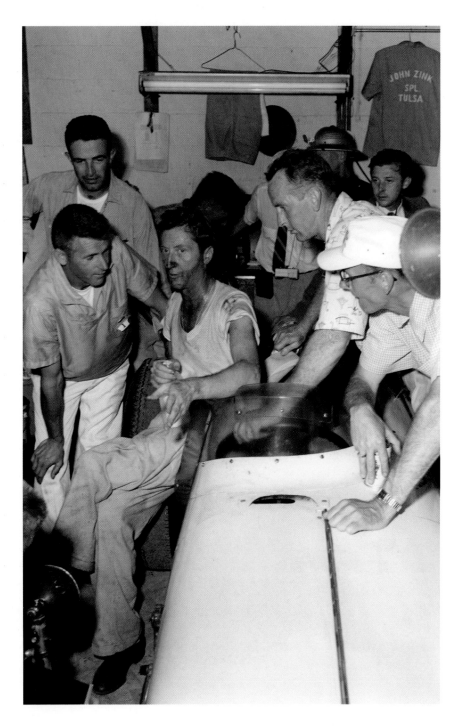

The Zink Racing team was well prepared to regroup and go forward. Watson was hailed as the "boy genius" for his new design. Flaherty emerged from the race ready for the next challenge. And Jack and John were described as the "new dynasty" in automobile racing. Fortunately, they had a healthy infusion of cash to build on that reputation. For the victory, they received an official purse of $93,819, which included $49,000 for coming in first, $1,500 as the fastest qualifier, $19,050 in lap prizes, and $23,375 from automotive accessory firms whose products were used in the race. Not counted were fees for personal appearances and endorsements, which usually doubled the cash won on the track. Even after sharing forty percent of the winnings with the driver and ten percent with the

Pat Flaherty (facing page, at left) and A.J. Watson (right), get a kiss from Virginia Mayo after coasting into Victory Lane.

A.J. Watson (left) with exhausted driver, Pat Flaherty, in the garage after the victory in 1956.

chief mechanic, Jack and John were well armed for the future. [25]

That future included more than the Indianapolis 500 and the Championship Series. Throughout the years of assembling a team for Indy, Jack kept a full stable of midget cars and stock cars at the local, state, and regional levels. With Dennie Moore building, maintaining, and managing the cars, Jack could play mechanic when he had time and even drive occasionally. By 1954 Jack and Dennie had two cars on the local tracks. For Tulsa they built what one reporter called a "much modified" Chevrolet coupe "that bellowed like a tractor." For the Oklahoma City track, they modified a 1950 Oldsmobile two-door sedan. On the same day that Bob Sweikert drove the John Zink Special to victory at Indy in 1955, Tulsa native Tommy Vardeman drove the Zink Chevy to victory in a seventy-five-minute marathon race at the Tulsa Fairgrounds. [26]

In the winter of 1955-56, Jack was asked to make a bid to manage the Tulsa Fairgrounds Speedway, which had slipped from an attendance of 135,000 fans in 1953 to 77,000 fans in 1955. Other bidders were Cameron Cline, who had won the contract the previous year, Jack's old friend Ervin Wolfe, who had managed the track previously, and KVOO-TV sportscaster, Jim Warren. Jack proposed that if he won the contract, the fair commission would receive twenty-five percent of net proceeds up to $70,000, with a sliding scale that advanced to thirty percent over $120,000. He also indicated that he would bring big-time racing to Tulsa as well as the weekly stock car racing from April through November. On February 20, 1956, fair park manager Clarence C. Lester announced that the Zink team would manage and promote the races. [27]

After the victory at Indy in May of 1956, Jack felt even more confident about bringing "big time" racing to Tulsa because he was about to field a car on the fledgling NASCAR circuit of late model stock cars. Jack contacted Bunky Knudson with the Pontiac Division of General Motors and worked out a deal to run stock Pontiacs on the increasingly popular circuit dominated by Fords, Chevrolets, and Chryslers. Pontiac would give him a car, access to parts, and promotional support. He would get the car ready to run and supply the driver and chief mechanic. By July the number "8" car was ready for the track, featuring a graphics package that read "John Zink Industrial Burners and Residential Heaters," and "Driver: Pat Flaherty." [28]

While showing the finished car to Knudson, Jack and Dennie explained what they had done to "enhance" its power. After testing a variety of parts, they found a set of exhaust headers that increased the power and durability of the engine, but there was a problem. The stock front end of a Pontiac sedan was not wide enough for the headers. They discovered that Pontiac manufactured a version of the car for ambulances, which had a wider front end for a bigger engine. They installed the "stock" ambulance A-frame and the exhaust headers fit. When the Pontiac officials noticed the wider stance, they asked what they could call it. Jack suggested they call it "a wide track Pontiac." [29]

With Indy winner Pat Flaherty behind the wheel, the new Zink Pontiac ran in NASCAR races at Milwaukee and Hammond, Indiana. Although Jack admitted publicly that the new car was "beset with minor problems," it ran the second fastest qualifying time at Milwaukee. Then Jack convinced NASCAR officials to bring their late model cars to Tulsa for a race. He guaranteed a $4,500 purse, announced that he would drive his own car, and scheduled the 100-mile NASCAR Grand National for Saturday night, August 4, 1956. Time trials would begin at 7:00 p.m., followed by the race at 8:30. On the Thursday before the race, Jack put his "wide track" Pontiac on display for the public to see in front of Megee's store at 514 South Main Street in downtown Tulsa. [30]

With 5,000 fans in the grandstand, the races were delayed when several drivers appeared late. After the time trials, some of the drivers claimed the track was too dusty, so it was sprayed with water, which caused another delay. Then it was too slippery for some, which caused yet another delay. When the race finally started, Fireball Roberts from Daytona Beach quickly broke away from the pack in his Ford, with Jack in his Pontiac close behind. As the leaders were about to lap the field, Lee Petty (father of NASCAR legend Richard Petty) peeled off into the pits, wrestled the red flag away from a track official, and started waving the other drivers off the track. As he said later, he thought the track was too dusty to be safe. A scuffle started but the race was cancelled after only thirty-two laps.

The John Zink Racing Team (facing page) was the first sponsor of a Pontiac in stockcar racing. Jack (center), seen here with friend and partner, Dennie Moore (right), occasionally drove on the NASCAR circuit.

Jack (working on the engine) and Dennie (in front of the car), installed an ambulance front-end on the car so they could use bigger headers for more power. They called it a "wide track Pontiac."

One reporter who witnessed the race suggested that Petty had another motive for the unprecedented stoppage. He was far back in the pack with little hope of finishing well. The night before, racing in Oklahoma City, he had not even finished. The reporter noted that Petty was in a close battle for the season points leadership and that another night of racing out of the finishers would hurt his chances for winning the championship. Jack, as the promoter, had to reimburse admissions to angry fans for the next two days and lost all of his investment for advertising and track preparation. Realizing he preferred designing, driving, and managing his own cars and drivers, Jack did not seek an extension of his management at the Tulsa track. [31]

In 1957, after Pontiac renewed its contract with the Zink Racing Team for another year, Jack and Dennie hauled one of the two new cars to Daytona Beach, where the big NASCAR race had been preceded since 1948 by a traditional timed event on the beach. The "flying mile" involved a running start on the sand, with the fastest car between two markers, one mile apart, to be named the winner. It was too much for Jack to resist. Jack and Dennie unloaded the car before daybreak and secretly tested the quality of the sand as well as the tires he should run. Fortunately, they did not hit any tourists sleeping on the beach and they got away before the police arrived.

On the day of the race, they unloaded again, this time in the light of day, and lined up on the part of the beach that had produced the best results. Jack watched his speedometer climb quickly until he hit 136.565 miles per hour, a new world record almost four miles per hour faster than the second place car. The owners of a Chrysler Hemi could not believe their machine was beaten, so they filed a protest. In what was called an "unusually thorough" inspection of the cylinder heads, it was found that one of the eight was a few thousandths of an inch oversize. As one historian wrote, "Zink got the 'you can't be a little bit pregnant lecture'," and the record was withdrawn only a few hours after it had been set. [32]

The Pontiac experiment continued for another year, running both USAC and NASCAR races with Jud Larson and Jimmy Reece behind the wheel. Although the results on the oval tracks did not meet Jack's expectations, the car provided a few thrilling moments. With Jack driving, the car won the quarter-mile stock car class at the Grand National Drag Race Championships held in Oklahoma City. Then they planned to travel south to Juarez, Mexico, for another attempt at the flying mile record, this time held on a section of the Pan American Highway. Due to a scheduling problem, they did not go. [33]

Pat Flaherty never had a chance to seriously test his abilities in the "wide track" Pontiac, despite his continued success representing the Zink Racing Team across the country. After his victory at Indy in 1956, the popular Irishman looked unstoppable in the Championship Series with a victory at Milwaukee in June and a fifth place finish at Darlington in July, which left him with a commanding lead in the USAC points championship. All he needed for the national championship was a respectable finish at Springfield. It was not to be. Switching to the Kurtis Kraft dirt car, Flaherty was driving well when a car in front of him went into a spin. He could not get clear, ran over the rear wheel, and flipped. Although he survived the crash, he had a crushed arm, a broken shoulder, a broken jaw, and a fractured skull. It was the only serious injury ever suffered in a Zink racecar and it almost ended Pat Flaherty's career. [34]

With Pat recovering and the car repaired, Jack offered the rest of the Championship Series to Jud Larson, a native of Texas one historian would later describe as "fun loving, wild, and talented." Jack had known the older man since the late 1940s, when Jud drove midget cars for the M.A. Walker team in Oklahoma City. A specialist on dirt, Jud drove well enough for Jack that season to earn a fourth place finish at the Hoosier Hundred and a first place finish at Sacramento. Jud also earned a place in the book of famous racecar quotes when he first met A.J. Watson. He walked up to the chief mechanic, who was working on the car, and said, "I'm Jud Larson...is this the s__t-box I'm supposed to drive?"[35]

Before the season ended, Jack and A.J. Watson were already looking ahead to the next Indy race and another effort to improve their mastery of speed and handling. For the 1957 Indy race, they went back to the drawing boards and built the second true "Watson roadster," which was five inches shorter than the 1956 winning car and another fifty pounds

Jack drove the Pontiac stockcar on the sands of Daytona Beach trying to set a new "flying mile" record. A film crew captured the moment as he accelerated to a speed of 136 miles per hour.

Troy Ruttman & Crew
Indianapolis Motor Speedway
=1957=

lighter, giving the car a boxier look. To shift even more weight onto the left front wheel, which tended to lift off the pavement in the turns, they mounted the oil tank on outriggers thrusting out from the body to the left. They also shifted the engine another inch to the port side, accentuating the off-center look of the car. [36]

In May of 1957, with Flaherty still recovering from his injuries, Jack put veteran Troy Ruttman behind the wheel of the new car as the team prepared for Indy. Jud Larson, who had driven so well the previous summer, was assigned to the 1956 Indy winning car even though he admittedly did not like the pavement of Indy. Then the bad luck that had started with Flaherty's crash returned. First, Larson could not get his qualifying speeds high enough and he was bumped from the field on the final weekend of qualifying. Then, the day before the race, Ruttman was taking practice laps when he put too much pressure on an experimental emergency brake. The wheel exploded, blew a tire, and sent the car into a spin. Fortunately, the damage was limited to the wheel, which was repaired in an amazingly quick thirty minutes, and the car and driver were back on the track. [37]

On race day the dark cloud over the team continued to cast a shadow. Ruttman, the only driver in the field who had won at Indy, was confident. He had a fast car that had qualified at 144.5 miles per hour, a good crew that was regularly completing practice pit stops in twenty-nine to thirty-two seconds, and the outside position on the front row, which many considered the best place to start a race. The confidence quickly turned to concern. During the pace lap, two cars collided, which forced a delay and an agonizingly slow pace as the cars crawled around the track a second time. When the race finally began, Ruttman shot into the lead and seemed to have plenty of power. Suddenly, smoke started coming from the engine but he continued the pace. After a few more laps the smoke increased and Ruttman pulled into the pits. Upon inspection, it was determined that the slow pace at the beginning of the race had damaged one of the pistons. After two consecutive victories, the Zink team dejectedly watched the race from the sidelines. [38]

After that anticlimactic beginning of the season, Jack regrouped and

The John Zink Race Team returned to Indy in 1957 with two cars, including number 5 with Troy Ruttman behind the wheel. Jack is fifth from the left.

sent his racing team back into battle. The winning car in the 1956 race continued on the Championship Series, first with Troy Ruttman in the cockpit, then with driver Jimmy Reece, who had been with Jack at that first Indy race in 1952. Troy finished tenth at Milwaukee and Jimmy took a respectable second, eighth, and fifth at the next three races. Then the battle went international when Jack accepted an invitation to race in a new 2.6 mile, high-banked oval in Monza, Italy. Designed to test the best cars and drivers of Europe and South America against the Americans, the inaugural 500-mile race did not attract the expected field, with the top European drivers saying it was too dangerous with expected average speeds of more than 160 miles per hour. Despite the European no-shows, Jack put Troy Ruttman in the new 1957 Watson Roadster and came in second, finishing fifth, second, and first in the three 166-mile-long heats. [39]

When the 1957 season ended, A.J. and Jack once again started reloading for the next Indianapolis 500. Their new car, slightly lighter with a lower profile to reduce drag, was assigned at Jack's insistence to Jimmy Reece, who pushed it to a qualifying time good for the coveted third spot on the first row. The unlucky car that had run for the first time at the Speedway in 1957 was initially assigned to a still recovering Pat Flaherty, but he failed his physical just a few weeks before the race. Taking his place was A.J.'s choice of drivers, Ed Elisian, a taciturn, 200-pound ex-gunner's mate from Oakland, California, who had never done very well at Indy. This time, in a Watson Roadster with Jack's team behind him, he looked like a champion and set a new Speedway qualifying record at 148.926 miles per hour. Also qualifying for the race on the seventh row was Jud Larson, driving the Zink racecar that had won at Indy in 1956. [40]

Despite the celebrated success of qualifying three cars for the race, the Zink Team still seemed to be under the dark cloud that had dogged them the previous year. The first bump in the road was the issue over who would drive the new Watson Roadster. Jack had promised the wheel to Jimmy, while A.J. had wanted his friend Elisian in the cockpit. The tension grew when Dick Rathmann, driving for the Lee Elkins Team, nudged Elisian from the pole position when he hit 148.974 in qualifying, a difference of only eight one-hundredths of a second. The real blow was not losing the pole position; it was the fact that the Elkins' car was designed and built by A.J. Watson, the salaried chief mechanic for the Zink Racing Team. [41]

TO INDY AND BEYOND: THE LIFE OF RACING LEGEND JACK ZINK

On race day, with that unsettling development lingering, the drivers squeezed into their cars and the race began. Jimmy, on the outside, calmly fell into third place as Elisian and Rathmann flew wheel-to-wheel around the first turn, down the straight-away, and into the second turn. On the third turn, with neither driver willing to back down, Elisian went into a spin, collected Rathmann, and both went head long into the wall. Jimmy, close behind on their tailpipes, anticipated the collision and tromped on his brakes, but he was instantly hit by another car, putting him into a spin. As he came around, he saw the car driven by Pat O'Connor coming right at him. When it hit the nose of his Zink Special, Jimmy ducked and the tire rolled over his shoulder, leaving a visible tread mark. O'Connor's car flipped end over end and came to rest upside down. The popular young driver was killed instantly. Elisian and Rathmann both walked away from the wreck, but they were out of the race along with six other cars. Larson, trailing the pack, drove into the infield and recovered, while Jimmy immediately limped into the pits. [42]

Jack, A.J., and Dennie quickly surveyed the damage. The headrest behind Jimmy's head was bent and twisted. The nosepiece was ripped and crushed. The right front wheel was bent and the tail was shattered. The fuel tank was twisted but there were no visible leaks. The team moved into action. As they cut and trimmed twisted metal, others started changing the damaged wheel when they saw that the steering draglink was bent into the body. Jack and A.J., according to a reporter serving on the pit crew, "used their bare hands to bend the heavy steel piece back into shape." In less than sixty seconds from when he pulled into the pits, Jimmy was back on the track as the field slowly advanced under the yellow caution flag. [43]

When the race resumed, Jimmy pushed his powerful car as if it had never been damaged. He worked his way up to seventh place, when suddenly a stream of oil started flowing from the engine into the cockpit. Covered in oil, Jimmy pulled into the pits and the crew once again started analyzing the problem. This time, after three minutes of a futile search, they shrugged and sent the car back onto the track. Miraculously, the oil leak stopped and Jimmy started the heartbreaking climb back through the field, this time starting in seventeenth place.

Jud Larson (facing page) was a racing veteran who drove Jack's second car in the 1957 Indy 500.

All was going well for the Oklahoma City driver when his tailpipe, broken in the initial crash, fell off. This changed the exhaust note of the car, and as Jimmy said later, he had "the appalling sensation that his engine was about to give up." Still, he flogged on, working his way through the competition lap after lap as he chased and then passed the leaders. When the checkered flag came down, however, race officials declared Jimmy Bryan the winner, less than a lap ahead of the hard-charging Reece, who came in sixth. Reece, with Jack's backing, afterward claimed that race officials had lost track of the cars after the disastrous first lap melee, and that Reece was not given credit for getting his car back on the track after the amazingly quick pit stop. Their pleas were overruled. Until his death in a crash a year later, Jimmy Reece believed that he had won the 1958 Indianapolis 500. [44]

His teammate, Jud Larson, who had started on the seventh row and been safely behind the fatal crash on the third turn, had several fast laps and fought some spirited duels. During one of his pit stops, the Zink crew changed tires and refueled the car in what one reporter called "an amazing twenty-four seconds," a new Speedway record. He finished in eighth place.[45]

Although disappointed and in some ways disillusioned, the Zink Racing Team went back into the garage and repaired the cars in preparation for the rest of the season. The second Watson Roadster, which had been driven by Ed Elisian in the heartbreaking first lap wreck, was handed to Jim Rathmann, who had done well at Indy in the past and finished second on the Championship Trail in 1957. His first assignment was a return trip to Italy for the Monza 500, billed as the "fastest auto race ever run." [46]

On June 29, 1958, A.J. and Jack watched their car line up against the best cars from the United States, Europe, and South America. Like the previous year, there were to be three heats around the 2.6-mile, steeply banked track. Rathmann started well and ran strong, winning the first heat with an average speed of 167.376, almost thirty miles per hour faster than the times at Indy. Then they won the second heat with a speed of 165.262, and followed with a victory in the third heat at 167.376, leading

Wearing their "Zink Pink" shirts (page 108), Jack and A.J. were the two-time reigning champs at Indy as they prepared for the 1957 race.

The Zink team had three cars in the race with Jack standing by the number 16 car (left, page 109).

TO INDY AND BEYOND: THE LIFE OF RACING LEGEND JACK ZINK

all but ten of the 189 laps. The victory, which won the team $40,000, was attributable to a combination of speed and durability. Of the nineteen cars that started the race, only six finished all three heats. [47]

Jack, who had been in Europe meeting with John Zink Company clients before the race, remained behind when the team departed for home. This time it was not business that kept him in Europe, but a chance to tour the Mercedes and Porsche manufacturing plants with Dr. Ferdinand Porsche, who had wanted to meet the two-time Indy 500-winning team owner. At the insistence of the famed car designer, Jack purchased a 1958 Porsche coupe, complete with a full set of metric tools. Forty years later, Jack would have it restored and placed next to his prized racecars along with the same set of metric tools. [48]

As the racing season continued over the summer, Jack and A.J. Watson continued to discuss their working relationship. For several years, Jack had been asking A.J. to move to Tulsa so they could work together more closely and consolidate the Zink Racing Team operations that were quickly expanding to multiple cars on the Championship Trail, Pontiacs in the NASCAR series, and numerous midget cars, stock cars, and off road vehicles. As early as 1956 A.J. publicly acknowledged that he would move, and he even sold his house in 1958, but each time he got close to the move, he backed out at the last minute. His future might be in Tulsa, but his heart was in Southern California. [49]

Jack steadily increased the pressure on A.J. to move for several reasons. First, Jack was traveling more than ever, representing the John Zink Company as he and his father expanded into overseas sales and manufacturing. By 1958 Jack was spending more than half of his professional life on the road. He also was recently married with his first child on the way. If he was to continue the expansion of the business, build a family life, and satisfy his passion for automotive engineering, he had to find a better way to balance his professional, personal, and racing responsibilities. He needed his chief mechanic in Tulsa.

This aerial photograph (facing page) illustrates the off-set position of the driver's seat, which was made possible by tilting the engine to run the drive shaft beside the driver instead of under him.

Dennie Moore (left, page 110) relaxes in front of the garage as cars move through "Gasoline Alley" for qualifying laps.

Jack (right, page 111) and A.J. put Ed Elisian behind the wheel in their new car for the 1957 race at Indy.

Perhaps even worse than the long-distance problem was the issue of A.J. building cars for other team owners. Since 1955 Jack had paid A.J. a weekly salary and given him a truck to haul the cars from race to race. To Jack, A.J. was an employee using Zink resources to design faster and lighter racecars. When a copy of one of the new cars was sold to a competing race team, Jack was, in the understated words of one historian, "not pleased," especially when that competing car won the pole position at Indy and was involved in the crash that took his best car out of the race. To A.J., he was following in the footsteps of other successful car designers who traditionally built cars for different teams. In his mind, he satisfied his commitment to Jack, then looked for additional opportunities to make a living. [50]

It was against this backdrop of tension between Jack and A.J. that, in June of 1958, the Zink team had traveled to Monza, Italy, and won the high-speed international race. This time, to help cover expenses, Jack had brought in as a partner, Bob Wilke, a long-time racing enthusiast who had recently purchased a greeting card company and was interested in putting together his own racing team. While they were in Italy celebrating their unprecedented success in winning all three heats at record speeds, Wilke asked A.J. if he would be his new chief mechanic. Just as importantly, he encouraged the young designer to build cars for other teams. On Labor Day of 1958, the winning team of Jack Zink and A.J. Watson ended after four years, two Indy 500 victories, and a place in the history books of big car racing. [51]

———∞∞———

To Jack, there was still much history to be written. He immediately pulled Oklahoma City native Dennie Moore from his stock car operations to run the Championship Trail series. He also changed drivers, replacing Jud Larson with Tony Bettenhausen, a native of Tulsa known as the "Tinley Park Express." Bettenhausen, described by Jack as "a delight to work with and very aggressive," quickly drove one of the Zink dirt track cars to a second place finish. In subsequent races he finished third, fifth, third, fifth, and second, winning the seasonal points championship even though he never won a race. As Jack would say many times, "to finish first, first you must finish." [52]

Jack and Dennie returned to the garage to design a new car for the upcoming 1959 season. The car, the first Indy-style car designed and built in Oklahoma, was appropriately emblazoned with a map of the state of Oklahoma on the hood when it first appeared on the track. To drive the car, Jack selected veteran Bob Veith, a native of California who had first raced at Indy in 1956. Veith, who had driven a Watson car for the Bob Estes team the previous year, called Jack's and Dennie's new ride "the best handling race car I've ever driven with power to match." At qualifying, Veith pushed the car to an average speed of 144.023, good enough for a spot on the third row. [53]

Jack also entered the Watson-designed roadster driven by Jimmy Reece the previous year. Tragically, Jimmy had since been killed while driving a car for another team, so the wheel was given to Pat Flaherty, who had won the big race in 1956 and was still recovering from his near fatal crash later that year. Flaherty qualified the car at 142.339 and earned a spot on the sixth row. "We have good cars, good drivers, and good mechanics," Jack said to the press. "Now, we'll have to wait until the race and see if we have good luck." [54]

The race started well for the Zink cars. Veith ran steadily, staying with the leaders for the first twenty laps before he fell back as the field stepped up the pace. He moved up to sixth place on the fiftieth lap, then dropped back to seventh, ninth, and tenth through the eightieth lap. Near the halfway mark, he made his best bid when he passed Duane Carter, Tony Bettenhausen, A.J. Foyt, Paul Russo, and Johnny Boyd to move into fifth place. At lap 160 he took a pit stop, lost a few spots, and worked hard to finish in ninth place. [55]

Flaherty, by contrast, drove more aggressively to the delight of the 185,000 fans at the Speedway. Starting in eighteenth place, the Chicago tavern owner quickly worked his way to the front pack and on the twenty-fourth lap began a furious battle for first place with Jim Rathmann, who was driving a similar Watson roadster. It was hub to hub for the next eighteen laps, with Flaherty staying on the accelerator deeper into the turns, and Rathmann making up the lost ground on the straight-aways.

One reporter, who had been to many races, wrote that it was "frightening to watch...several racing veterans described it as the most exciting contest they had ever witnessed." Then, lady luck turned. [56]

On his first pit stop, all went well as the practiced Zink team put in fifty gallons of fuel and changed three tires in less than twenty seconds. When Flaherty started back onto the track, however, he heard a crack as he lost second gear. On the second pit stop, without the starting gear, the engine stalled and precious seconds were lost as the team unsuccessfully tried to push start the car and then returned it to the pits to use the mechanical starter. Back on the track, Flaherty roared into the thick of the fight but he was visibly tiring. [57]

Jack, knowing that the long two-year layoff had taken a toll on his driver, found a back up driver to take over as the race approached the 140th lap. But when Flaherty pulled into the pits for his third and final stop, he refused to give way. Minutes later, disaster struck. "I was coming out of the fourth turn onto the main straight behind another car when he suddenly slowed down as if his engine had gone bad," reported Flaherty. "To keep from hitting him I turned sharply to the inside. Normally, I would have corrected and gone on, but my reflexes were just a fraction too slow and the car went into a spin." Flaherty kissed the outside wall several times, skidded across the track, and hit the inside wall. He emerged from the wreck with only bruises, but the car was out of the race. [58]

The next two years at Indy ended with similar disappointments. In 1960 Troy Ruttman, a native of Mooreland, Oklahoma, took the wheel of the Watson roadster and qualified in sixth place, but retired from the race after 128 laps with a broken gear in the rear end. The next year Ruttman drove the car designed by Dennie Moore and qualified on the eighth row, but again had mechanical problems when a clutch failed on the 105th lap.

Despite such setbacks, the Oklahoma contingent still had fun. Jack's father, John, hosted more than 300 guests under a 40-by-120 foot circus tent pitched in the shadows of the famous Speedway. For three days the self-proclaimed "Okies" slept on cots, enjoyed the gourmet cooking of Tulsa chef Earl Davis, and surrendered to John's fun-loving

Even though 1956 would be their last checkered flag at Indy, Jack and Dennie continued with their innovative design concepts for years afterward. The external oil tank shown here (facing page) improved this car's balance.

spirit. One reporter described the elder Zink as "the man who gets the biggest kick out of them all...with a kid's happy grin on his face as he strides through the tent wearing a pith helmet and terry cloth shorts, swinging a heavy cane. This is his kind of fun and he squeezes pleasure out of every second of it."[59]

With a similar intensity, Jack regrouped after the disappointing finish and dedicated his team to getting back to Victory Lane. But this time, he was determined to get there a different way, an engineer's way of mixing up old formulas, calculating new innovations, and applying theoretical concepts to working machines. No longer was incremental change enough. No longer would he be satisfied with another team's design. What Jack Zink wanted was something no one had ever done before, so revolutionary that it would turn the racing world on its head. Jack wanted to be the first to race a turbine engine at the Indianapolis 500 Speedway.

—◦◦◦—

Jack's interest in the turbine engine dated to the winter of 1955-56, when he test drove the experimental car being developed by the Air Force. Following that revelation, in 1956 he heard a presentation titled, "Gas Turbine Competition at Indianapolis," by Leonard H. Williams, an industrial engineer at the Boeing Aircraft Company of Seattle, Washington. "The turbine has been proven to be far more reliable than the conventional piston engine," Williams said, "but people resist change." To Jack Zink, change was a way of life in the field of industrial burners and essential in the pursuit of profit through adaptation and problem solving. [60]

The turbine was not the only innovation embraced by Jack Zink and Dennie Moore. Since 1956, the two constants in the evolution of racecar design had been the reduction of weight and the elimination of drag by lowering the profile of the body. A.J. Watson's success was not a new design, but rather the elimination of 200 pounds and a slightly lower ride. In Europe, where Jack was busy expanding the industrial reach of the John Zink Company, he had many opportunities to witness the speed and agility of Grand Prix-style cars that were even lighter and closer to the ground. If he could find a way to strengthen the sleeker, lighter body

design of those Grand Prix cars to withstand the rigors of the 500-mile oval at Indy, Jack would gain still another advantage.

During the winter months of 1960, Jack and Dennie started experimenting with the lighter, Grand Prix-style body. Jack did the design, completing all the drawings and often working through the night and sleeping the next day on an airplane. Dennie fabricated the pieces and assembled the chassis, while Tulsa native Carl Oliver fashioned the sleek body with the cockpit pushed to the front of the car and the driver's feet in the nose. The revolutionary new car was ready for its maiden shakedown in July of 1961. Although designed for a turbine, the car was tested with a traditional Offenhauser and journeyman driver "Big Bill" Cheesebourg at the wheel. As he got the hang of the car, he turned in several laps at 138 miles per hour, fast enough to have qualified for the 1959 race. After cutting the fast laps, the driver told Dennie "I wasn't even pushing hard." They left the test drives with plans to adjust wheel camber and caster, incorporate offset weight distribution for the left hand turns at Indy, and soften the steering, which was too quick for the Speedway. [61]

The tougher challenge was the turbine engine. On the upside, the turbine was simple and reliable, with only seven moving parts, plus it turned out a tremendous amount of torque. Even more important to Jack, a turbine weighing less that an Offy could turn out more than twice the horsepower. On the downside, it was a gas guzzler, getting less than three miles to the gallon, which would require bigger fuel tanks and added weight. And although the turbine ran well at high speeds, it accelerated slowly coming out of the turns, taking as much as seven seconds to go from idle to the 39,000 rpms required for straight-aways. By contrast, the traditional Offys needed less than one second to recover. As the 1961 Memorial Day race approached, those problems were still not solved, so the new rear engine car sat in the garage while a new traditional roadster carried the Zink banner. Unfortunately, after 105 laps, the car was retired with a clutch problem and did not finish the race. [62]

Back in their Tulsa shops, Jack, Dennie, and the engineers from Boeing worked on an innovative "waste gate" that would allow the turbine to run at a constant, full-throttle speed, while simply opening the gate to

Jack's proud father John (facing page) stands in-between one of the race cars and a new motor coach that he used to attend races.

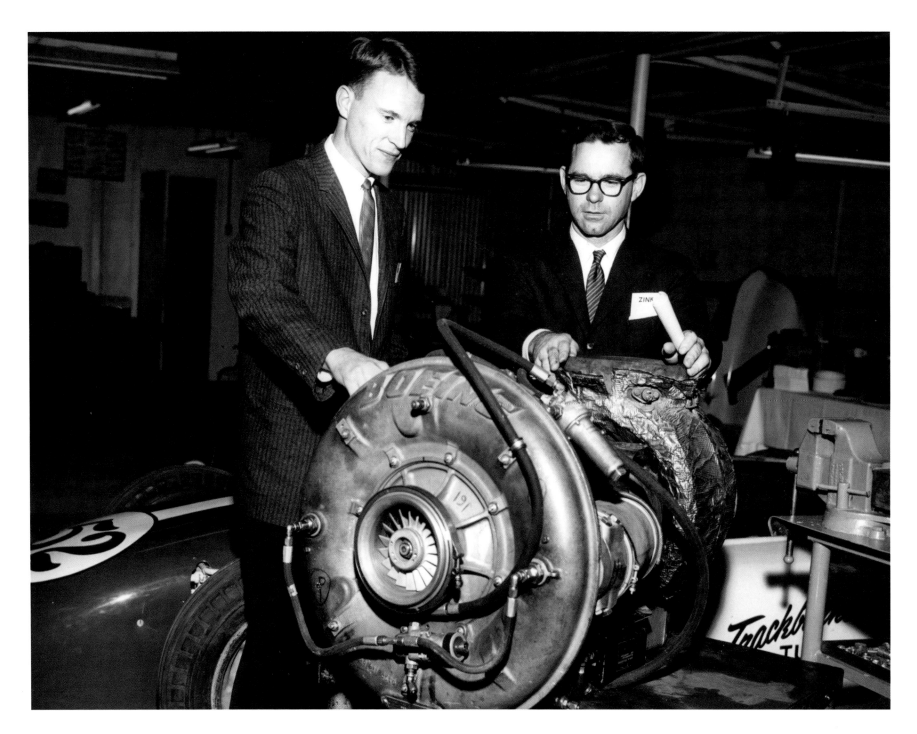

TO INDY AND BEYOND: THE LIFE OF RACING LEGEND JACK ZINK

divert propelling turbine gasses away from the drive shaft mechanism so the driver could back off going into the turns. Closing the gate, conversely, would put the full force of the gasses back in operation and give the car instantaneous acceleration. An additional challenge was the sloshing action of the sixty-three-gallon fuel tanks, which affected handling. Jack and the team developed a baffling system within the tanks to solve that problem.[63]

The waste gate solution was not so successful. Despite all the hard work, the gate did not divert all of the gasses from the drive mechanism and there was 100 horsepower that could not be eliminated. The troublesome propulsion pushed the racer into the curves too fast. Jack, who was doing the test driving on a half-mile track, told one reporter that the extra power forced him to "brake like mad and the brake cylinders got so hot they were glowing red." They finally retreated and significantly modified the waste gate in the spring of 1962, adding a new throttle assembly that required the driver to follow a precise formula of timing and tachometer readings to manipulate the curves. Always the optimist, Jack told one reporter that the modifications in the waste gate got the weight of the turbine down to 335 pounds, more than 200 pounds lighter than the Offy.[64]

On May 3, 1962, Jack was testing the turbine-powered car when the new assembly stuck in the closed position. Under full power, the car roared off the track, hit a ditch, and flipped over twice before it landed upright. Crew members rushed to the car and pulled Jack out before a fire started. The car miraculously suffered little damage, limited to a bearing carrier on the rear axle, which was immediately ordered and installed. Jack was taken to the hospital and treated for face lacerations and a severely cut lip. Within two days, Jack was back in the garage and the car was on a trailer being towed to the Speedway.[65]

Named the "Trackburner," the turbine-powered car was the talk of the town. The scheduled driver was Dan Gurney, a rookie at the Speedway who had gained fame racing on the European circuits. When he got to the track, Gurney passed his rookie test in the Zink roadster, then started practicing in the Trackburner. It did not go well. Although the car had good acceleration coming out of the turns, it was underpowered in the straight-aways. Jack told a reporter that he had wanted the newest

Boeing 520 engine that produced 500 horsepower, but it had not been finished in time. Instead, he had to use the 375-horsepower Boeing 502. To compound the problem, the weather during qualifying was hot and humid, which further reduced the power of the turbine.

Although he had pushed the revolutionary car to a respectable lap at an average of 145 miles per hour, Gurney grew more nervous about the experimental nature of what they were doing and jumped to another team. The turbine car was given to Duane Carter, a track veteran who also recorded a few laps that averaged more than 140 miles per hour, probably good enough to make the field of thirty-three cars. But Jack was not willing to "just" make the field with no chance of winning, so he withdrew the Trackburner without attempting to qualify. Carter moved over to the Zink roadster and was running well in qualifying when a crankshaft failed on his final lap. For the first time since 1949, the 1962 Indianapolis 500 would be run without an entry affiliated with the Zink name.[66]

As the disappointment of the turbine experiment sunk in, a reporter asked Jack if he had given up his role as auto racing's chief proponent of experimentation. "Yes," he answered, "but only temporarily." With the allure of racing strong as ever, Jack would return to the Speedway, but in the meantime, there were other mountains to climb. Still only thirty-three years old, time was on his side.

With veteran driver Dan Gurney (facing page), Jack inspects the Boeing gas turbine engine he was trying to adapt to car racing.

Changing Gears

"I believe in short term pain for long term gain."
Jack Zink

C H A P T E R   F I V E

Once again, Jack Zink faced a turning point in his life. After twice capturing the Indianapolis 500 and taking the racing world by storm, he found himself on top of the highest mountain where simply winning was not enough. He had to break new ground, explore uncharted waters, accomplish something no one had ever done before. The turbine engine experiment, one of the most radical departures from tradition in the history of car racing, had motivated him like few other challenges, but the failure to achieve his own self-imposed standards left him dazed and unsure of his future in the sport.

There also were changes in his family life. After the birth of three sons, Neel, Colin, and Whitney, Jack and his first wife, Ellen, were divorced in 1962. If he was to be a part of his sons' lives, he had to restructure his time to take them sailing on weekends, watch them play baseball, and lead them on adventures such as rafting expeditions through the Grand Canyon. On top of that was the changing management partnership with his father at the John Zink Company.

In 1962 John Steele Zink was sixty-nine years old and in poor health. He still went to the office every day, but usually for only an hour or two to check on his investments and stay in close touch with his fiercely loyal employees. Instead, his creative energies were spent on the Zink Ranch. In 1946, when his foundry burned to the ground, John had taken the insurance settlement and purchased a picturesque parcel of land in Osage County only twenty-six miles from the heart of downtown Tulsa. Over the next sixteen years, at first paying as little as three to seven dollars an acre, he followed with another sixty-eight land transactions as he built the family holdings to more than 10,000 acres. At first he looked for a practical use of the land. "I was camped up here one night," he told a reporter, "and I heard the Lord talking to me. He said, 'John, you've got all this land so you'd better put some cattle on it.' So I started buying cattle and three years later I figured I had lost something like $150,000 on them and I heard the Lord talking to me again. He said, 'John, get out of the cattle business. You don't know anything about it.' "[1]

Improving the Zink Ranch became John's passion. He built a hangar-like building measuring 100-by-160 feet, which he named "The Rendezvous." As he told a reporter, it was a "poor man's country club," decorated with bunk beds, rustic furniture, and all the trappings of a hunting and fishing lodge. In 1961, wanting private sleeping quarters, he purchased an aging fifty-six-foot-long house trailer and asked his employees from the plant to hoist it on top of the hunting lodge.[2]

John's "outings" quickly gained fame. Even in the summertime, the oversized fireplace blazed away because he liked the sound and smell of burning firewood. One evening guests arrived to find him sitting with a muzzled alligator in his lap and rattlesnakes in a nearby box. Another evening a United States Supreme Court Judge was a guest. To add some life to the party when the conversation lagged, John unleashed a raccoon in the lodge and set his pack of dogs on the trail.[3]

An avid sportsman, John built a rifle range on the Zink Ranch with targets at 100, 200, and 300 yards. The fifty-bench facility was described in the September, 1956 issue of *Precision Shooting Magazine* as the "nation's best bench rest shooting range," which he readily shared with local shooting clubs and troops of Boy Scouts. To make the far reaches of the ranch

Jack (page 120) with the rear engine, Grand Prix-style car he designed for the Championship Series. Jack balanced his business career in the 1950s and 1960s with racing and family (above and facing page).

Grandpa John Steele Zink with his grandsons and their friends.

accessible to visitors, he bought a $32,450 Model D7E Caterpillar bulldozer and a $29,000 grader and started moving dirt, boulders, and trees. With the same intensity he had used to create his company three decades earlier, he built more than thirty miles of road, dozens of ponds, and a replica of a frontier boom town for the Boy Scouts. [4]

John could focus on the Zink Ranch because his son, Jack, was increasingly assuming a leadership role in running the John Zink Company. In 1962 Jack was thirty-four years old, a gifted engineer with a number of patents to his credit, and a tireless workaholic who rose early, stayed up late, and spent almost half of his time each year on the road representing the company and generating new business. As he traveled, he learned, negotiating with executives in front offices and collaborating with engineers and facility managers in plants. Jack recognized the value of this apprenticeship, telling a reporter, "That's one of the advantages of a father-son business. You can take the time you need to travel and know that nobody is stealing the business while you're gone." [5]

As Jack grew into the leadership role, the business itself was changing. In 1949, the year before Jack graduated from Oklahoma A&M, the John Zink Company made most of its money by manufacturing consumer products such as room fans, attic fans, space heaters, and its nationally known floor furnaces, which were sold in all forty-eight states. In 1952 the company even expanded its consumer line by entering the infant residential market for water-cooled air conditioning units. Working with a Tulsa developer who promised to air condition ninety-five homes in a new housing addition at 31st and Yale, the company produced a five-ton unit for houses of more than 1,500 square feet and a three-ton unit for smaller homes. [6]

The sale of industrial burners, which had been the bedrock product of the company in 1930, lagged behind, due partly to the depression in the oil patch across the Southwest and partly to the fact that the company had no trained engineers to develop the product line. When Jack joined the company in 1950, his first assignment was to get into the field, find customers, and come up with burner applications that would create jobs and profits back in Tulsa. What followed was the development of the industry's first test furnace, the inauguration of the first "burner schools," the invention of smokeless flares, and the application of high intensity burners to the production of specialty items such as hydrazine, the fuel used by NASA to power the first manned space flights.

As if reflecting the changes in the lives of John and Jack, the company was at a crossroads as well. The market for Zink consumer products was declining, especially for the bread-and-butter line of floor furnaces, which were being replaced by central heat and air units in new homes. At the same time, the market for industrial burners was growing, not so much in the old familiar haunts of Tulsa and the American Southwest, but more so in the national and international markets where new sources of oil and gas were being discovered and processed. With John semi-retired and spending more time at the ranch, Jack was called on to guide the company through this new era of transition and expansion.

❧

John enjoyed his D9 caterpillar bulldozer (facing page), successor to his D7E dozer. He shared these toys with Jack and his grandsons at the Zink Ranch.

Jack realized that the company either had to streamline and focus on a declining but specialized market niche or expand into new products and new markets, especially overseas. There was no in-between. It was either play it safe and maximize profits on declining sales or take a chance and jump into the major leagues where failure was a realistic possibility. For Jack, who had balanced courage with caution at the highest levels of car racing, the safe route was not an option. If he could not be first, he would look for a different game.

To reach international markets, Jack knew he had to accomplish two goals. One was to develop field representatives who could take the pressure off of him to be everywhere and be a part of every relationship. "We've got a product," he told a reporter, "but we sell a service." Two, he had to find a way to cut through import restrictions in countries where native firms had an advantage. The solution was to establish wholly-owned subsidiaries under his control but staffed by local businessmen. In 1960 the first such subsidiary was planted in Mexico, where the government-owned oil company, Pemex, was rapidly developing oil fields and refineries. When Pemex defaulted on its debts, the Mexican government turned to investors in England,

During the 1950s and 1960s Jack (left, below, and facing page) expanded the reach of the John Zink Company to international markets in Mexico, England, France, Germany, and Japan.

who extended new credit but demanded that all oil field and industrial purchases come from British companies. Jack quickly established a wholly-owned subsidiary in a suburb of London. The strategy worked. By November of 1963, the John Zink Company was selling more than a fourth of its products outside the United States, with manufacturing or sales branches in London, Paris, Frankfurt, and Milan. In 1964 Jack added Japan to the list as he traveled to twenty-two countries in one year. [7]

The growth of business in England serves as a good example of how the new markets developed. For decades, British housewives had used stoves fueled with "town's gas," a manufactured substitute for natural gas that was more expensive to use. With a Zink-designed burner, a new process was found to convert naphtha, plentiful in England, into a much cheaper gas. As town after town converted to the cheaper fuel, new burners were needed to build conversion plants. Virtually every unit came from the John Zink Company, "much to the dismay of some British manufacturers," reported John Corble, manager of the London office. In January of 1965, the British subsidiary moved into a new manufacturing plant built on 1.5 acres in St. Albans, Hertfordshire, a suburb of London. Two years later, the plant was expanded by another 9,000 square feet of space with a full-time staff of eighty. [8]

While overseas operations expanded, Jack led an equal effort to expand both consumer and industrial sales in America through the mid-1960s. On the consumer side, sales increased for refrigerated air conditioning units, first patented by the John Zink Company in 1958. At first, the main customers were developers and plumbers rushing to satisfy the demand for suburban homes across the South. During the early 1960s, it was common for one developer in a town like Tulsa or Oklahoma City to build 500 to 1,000 homes a year, each one equipped with a John Zink air conditioning unit.

In 1969 Jack expanded the air conditioning venture into commercial markets with units as large as fifteen tons. He built a 5,000-square-foot testing facility at the Peoria Street plant, where he told reporters, "testing will take all of the guesswork out of our products." As he had done almost two decades earlier with test furnaces for industrial burners, he and the engineers at the plant constructed a "hot room," a "cold room," and an instrumentation center where precise measuring equipment was installed to perform tests prescribed by the American Gas Association, Underwriters' Laboratories, and the American Refrigeration Institute. In one interview, Jack described how they had run an air conditioning unit in the 125-degree "hot room" for twenty-four hours. "There was no decline in efficiency," he reported. [9]

The new industrial cooling units were intended for stores, theaters, churches, and schools. Again breaking new ground in the business, Jack and his engineers designed a "completely factory-fabricated packaged unit that could be installed quickly and easily." According to Jack, the innovation could save customers up to fifty percent on the costs of installation. Other methods of keeping the costs down included long production runs on standard-sized units and a pre-fabricated base called a "Duct-Pak" that could be installed on the roof of a building to provide both an air supply and a filtered return for efficient circulation. As Jack told a group of reporters touring the plant, "it's just a matter of putting your engineering and manufacturing resources to work finding new answers to the problem." This same approach to solving problems opened doors to a new application for industrial burners in the 1960s. That new field was pollution control. [10]

The increasing awareness of pollution that had emerged during the

As environmental standards became more restrictive, Jack helped the John Zink Company dominate the design, construction, and installation of flares, including this elevated flare at a refinery.

1950s evolved into increasingly stringent local, state, and federal regulations in the 1960s as people recognized the economic and social impact of industrial waste on air, water, and soil. On land, the most visible problem was solid waste, the byproducts of consumerism and manufacturing that had to be buried in landfills or incinerated. Along rivers and coastal areas, the major problem was dumping untreated toxic waste into water supplies. In the industrial sector, where chemical processes often included the conversion of organic compounds through the application of heat, the biggest challenge was the discharge of pollutants into the atmosphere.

In Los Angeles air quality was so bad that violators of new anti-pollution standards were faced with plant closings as they struggled with "new laws with sharp teeth." When a plant owner was told he had only a few weeks to reduce pollutants or close, Jack and his team went into action. Engineers in Los Angeles fed information to Jack by phone, while workers at the Tulsa plant worked around the clock testing designs and building the equipment. Within two weeks of the initial telephone call, the unit was on a truck bound for California. Within another two weeks it was installed, one of the first hazardous waste incinerators in the nation. Soon thereafter, a similar unit was shipped the other direction for installation on a Goodrich Chemical Company plant in Calvert City, Kentucky. In both cases, the innovative new equipment kept workers employed and production running while meeting the new air quality standards. [11]

In 1965 leaders in the Great Lakes area convened a "Lake Erie Conference on Water Pollution" and asked Jack to attend. During the conference, Standard Oil Chemical Company announced that a "Zink Thermal Oxidizing System" was being installed at its Lima, Ohio acrylonitrile plant. Built at a cost of $500,000, the oxidizing units were 100-feet-tall and burned enough gas each year to meet the average requirements of a city of 40,000 people. After the units were up and running, Standard Oil officials announced that effluents dumped from their plant into the Ottawa River were free of organic chemical toxins. [12]

By the mid-1960s increased sales of anti-pollution oxidizers, ever more efficient burners, and bigger and better residential air conditioners and furnaces forced John and Jack to increase manufacturing capacity. First, they expanded the original plant on Peoria Avenue in Tulsa, which included the construction of a high-bay section where large units could be

Jack and his team of engineers tested a wide range of burners at the company plant in Tulsa (above and below). They were especially skillful at configuring flares that used steam injection to eliminate smoke (page 130).

assembled. Then they built a new 36,000-square-foot plant on the outskirts of the town of Skiatook in nearby Osage County, where sixty highly skilled welders and steel workers assembled huge incinerators. Within two years this plant was expanded by another 72,000 square feet as business continued to boom.

In 1969 Jack created a "Pollution Research Division." Robert Reed, the vice president for engineering, proudly announced that the new division included specialists who could deal with pollution problems in chemistry, chemical kinetics, physics, refractories and insulation, steel structures, diffusion, and smokeless flaring. "Industry needs help," Reed said, "and that is the purpose of our organization." For the next decade a continuous flow of drums containing samples of toxic waste arrived at the Zink plant in Tulsa where the test furnaces and related equipment were kept busy developing safe methods of disposal. [13]

Jack was on top of the business world. He was president of the John Zink Company, called by one magazine the largest privately owned company west of the Mississippi River. He was a recognized pioneer in the field of mechanical engineering, with more than twenty patents to his name. And his team of 600 employees spanned the globe with two manufacturing plants in Oklahoma, smaller plants in England and France, and sales offices in Houston, New York, Los Angeles, Germany, Italy, and Japan. [14]

To most people, growing an international business at a rate of fifteen percent a year with annual revenues of $50 million would have been enough of a challenge during the 1960s. Jack Zink, however, was not "most people." After failing to run a car in the 1962 edition of the Indianapolis 500, he was determined to get back to the top of the racing world. He still needed the challenge of speed.

Jack (above) used racing to build the John Zink Company. Here, he allows a client to sit in his Indy car for a photograph, one of thousands that Jack would give to friends and visitors over the years.

Dennie Moore (below) became the chief mechanic and Jack's partner in race car design after the split with A.J. Watson.

———

After experiencing the heart-breaking failure of their bold turbine experiment, which rendered them mere spectators at the big race in 1962, Jack and Dennie Moore shook the dust of disappointment from their boots and decided to retire the turbine-powered car. Instead, they returned to the Speedway in 1963 with a conventional roadster built by Dennie and Carl Oliver. As if to break the connection with the past, Jack came up with a new name, the "Zink Trackburner Sooner Sizzler." When

asked about the tongue twister, Jack responded, "we wanted a name that would identify our cars with Oklahoma." [15]

The team's new driver was Lloyd Ruby, a native of Wichita Falls, Texas, whom Jack called a "dandy who drives with his head as well as his foot." The team was working well together when disaster struck during a practice run on May 11, 1963. Speeding through the front turn at 140 miles per hour, Ruby's front right wheel shattered, sending him headlong into the wall. Ruby escaped with only minor injuries, but the car was demolished. Dennie quickly resurrected the ill-fated roadster built for the 1962 race that had failed to make the starting line when the crankshaft broke on the final qualifying lap. This time, the car ran well enough with Ruby on board to win a spot on the sixth row with a qualifying speed of 149.124. [16]

Ruby fulfilled Jack's high expectations. He started well back in the pack but steadily worked his way through the leaders until he was in third place and running strong. On lap 126, as the field started up after a yellow flag, he was barreling into the fourth turn just before the main straight away when he hit a patch of oil. He went into a spin, hit the outside wall, and careened into the infield where he came to a halt. He was out of the race. Later, a number of drivers complained that the winning car driven by Parnelli Jones was losing a steady stream of oil. No action was taken. [17]

Jack was disappointed with the crash, but his dissatisfaction went beyond the results of one race. It had been seven years since they had tasted sweet victory at the Speedway, and keeping a team at the leading edge of innovation was becoming increasingly expensive. Compounding the problem was Jack's rugged schedule at the John Zink Company, which kept him on the road half the year. Less time, more money, and an undiminished passion for innovation and technical perfection was not a formula that worked well in the challenging sport of open wheeled racing. Something had to give.

Into this dilemma stepped Charles Urshel, Jr., and Earl Slick, two oilmen and native Oklahomans who lived in San Antonio, Texas. The wealthy partners wanted to get into Indy-style racing, and Bill Jones, one of their employees, suggested they start by calling Jack, his longtime friend and

A tire gets away as the Zink Race Team (left) changes tires and refuels during a pit stop on the Championship Series. Jack (facing page) handled the fuel line during a pit stop at the Indianapolis 500.

CHANGING GEARS

winner of two races at the Speedway. Urshel and Slick asked Jack if he would go back to Indy with partners to share fifty percent of the costs. Jack responded that he would if they could go with a Formula One-type car similar to the body he had designed for the turbine experiment in 1960. They met in San Antonio, went out to dinner, and discussed options for the kind of car that could win at the Speedway. At the end of the meeting, they shook hands and a new partnership was formed. [18]

The next step was to find a veteran designer who knew the subtleties of the European racing machines. At the top of the list was Jack Brabham, a native Australian living in England better known as the driver who had twice won the World Road Racing Championship. Successful on the tracks of Europe, he had gone into the design and chassis building business and earned a reputation as an innovator open to new ideas. This was the combination Jack was looking for. They met several times, worked out a partnership that included Brabham as the driver, and started planning for the coming season. [19]

Brabham designed the chassis, while Jack and Dennie supplied the engine and put together the support team. The result was a sleek, cigar-shaped rear engine car that weighed about 1,250 pounds even with the husky Offenhauser engine, compared to the average weight of an American-built roadster at 1,700 pounds. The advantage, however, came at a price. On the Grand Prix circuit, cars ran shorter distances on flat, curved roads that favored nimble handling and quick acceleration. On American tracks, especially the Indianapolis Speedway, the race was longer and faster with a premium on brute power and durability.

The Zink-Urshel-Slick Trackburner was a pioneering attempt to bridge those two styles of racing, and as with any experimentation, problems arose almost daily. After the car arrived in America, Jack and Dennie immediately started modifying the chassis, usually without the input of Brabham, who was busy racing in Europe. They never did work out all the handling problems. Then disaster struck the team as they stood in the pits during a qualifying run. A two-pound, three-pronged wing nut from the front wheel of a car blazing down the track at 180 miles per hour came

Jack (left) was generous in allowing his race cars to draw crowds for all kinds of fund raisers and special events in Tulsa. With a full display of the team's cars at the John Zink Company plant, Jack (facing page) introduced his driver, Jim McElreath, to friends and clients.

off and hit Dennie on the back. No bones were broken, but he was incapable of continuing his duties as chief mechanic. In his place, Jack added Clint Brawner, a native of Arizona whose car was already out of the race. Although Brabham qualified the car at a speed of 152.04, good enough for a spot on the ninth row, the team was not happy with the handling all the way up to race day. [20]

When the 1964 race began, the leaders bolted to a quick pace, but Brabham could not stay with them. It took several laps for him to get up to 140 miles per hour, and even then he could not sustain the speed. On the third lap he met near disaster when a wreck engulfed the leaders, killing Eddie Sachs and rookie Dave MacDonald. Brabham drove around the pileup but a piece of another car ripped through the nose of the Trackburner. When track officials conducted an inspection, crewmember Bill Jones saw a drip of fuel hitting the pavement under the car. He tossed a rag over it, giving the crew members time to do their own inspection. They decided to keep going.

Brabham pushed the sleek car around the track until the seventy-seventh lap, when he abruptly came into the pits and frantically jumped out of the car. In the floorboard was a deepening pool of fuel leaking from tanks too light for the rugged conditions at the Speedway. The car was out of the race. Dennie, frustrated at their inability to solve the technical problems of running a Grand Prix car on the track at Indy, told one reporter that they should have gone with the traditional roadster sitting in their shops back in Tulsa. "If we'd brought that car, I'll bet you it would still be out there running." Jack, however, was not there just to finish; he wanted to win, and he knew that the old technology could not keep up. He was intent on pushing the envelope of innovation and getting back into Victory Lane. [21]

Despite the shortcomings of the Brabham design, there was hope. Clint Brawner, the substitute chief mechanic who had filled in for the injured Dennie Moore, thought they were on the right track. After Indy they added new and stronger fuel tanks, modified the suspension system, and adjusted the steering. They also added horsepower to the four-cylinder Offenhauser, even though new, more powerful Ford V-8s were rapidly taking over the racing world team by team. The work paid off. At Trenton in late June, the Zink-Urshel-Slick car led the race for a while, set a new course speed record, but dropped out with rear-end failure. The next year,

Jack's last car to make the starting line up at the Indianapolis 500 ran the 1966 race with an Offenhauser (above) and in 1967 with a Ford (facing page). One of Jack's team members was Bob DeBisschop (below), who specialized in getting the maximum power and performance out of engines.

To Jack Zink
Bob De Bisschop with
Turbo Offy He Developed - 1967

after recovering from a wreck in October that both demolished the car and injured the new driver, the car continued its improved performance with a second place finish in a 200-mile Championship race at Phoenix and a victory at Trenton. [22]

The new driver was Jim McElreath, a big, burly man from Arlington, Texas, who had first raced at Indy in 1962 when he was named "Rookie of the Year" at the age of thirty-two. As the Zink-Urshel-Slick Team approached the 1965 Memorial Day classic, McElreath was among the leaders for the season points Championship, but once again, misfortune dogged them. Two weeks before the race, an engine blew as they prepared for qualifying. Dennie and his crew quickly rebuilt and installed the spare engine in time for McElreath to qualify on the fifth row. On race day the car ran well until rear end gears stripped on the sixty-sixth lap. It was back to the garage. McElreath would go on to place third in the seasonal point standings in 1965, finishing behind Mario Andretti and A.J. Foyt. [23]

Meanwhile, Jack and his team continued to make major modifications to the fragile Brabham design at their shops next to the John Zink Company plant in Tulsa. The biggest change was a new engine, a Ford V-8 that produced about ten percent more horsepower, which was further modified by Dennie Moore, who designed and installed a new set of valves. Jack, who had been using the proven Offys since 1947, said "the switch was inevitable...the Ford's superior horsepower makes it virtually unbeatable." The only problem with the $20,000 Ford engine was rod bolt failure, which had sidelined fifteen of the thirty Fords on the Championship circuit the previous year. When the same problem struck the Trackburner, Jack worked with Tulsa metallurgist Warren Franks to come up with a better bolt. Their solution was a bolt made with rolled threads instead of conventional cut threads. The new design, common in the aviation industry, produced a bolt that could lift the weight of five full-sized automobiles. [24]

The new Tulsa-built Trackburner won in its first race as the 1966 season began. At Phoenix International Raceway, McElreath took the lead on the fortieth lap and was never seriously threatened. "We've got ourselves a winner here," said the happy driver after the 150-mile race. That confidence rose as the team prepared for their return to the Indianapolis Speedway. [25]

McElreath qualified at the Speedway with an average speed of 160.908, good enough for a spot on the third row behind Mario Andretti,

Lloyd Ruby, Parnelli Jones, and Gordon Johncock. On the pace lap, a crash took out eleven cars, followed by a series of mishaps that steadily reduced the number of cars on the track. Twice McElreath escaped near misses. First, Jim Clark went into a spin, forcing the big Texan to brake and duck onto the apron of the track to avoid a collision. Later, the Zink pilot was barreling around the track when he saw Al Unser's car lose a tire. "I thought the tire was coming into the car with me," McElreath said later. To avoid the tire, he braked, went into a spin, and recovered on the infield.[26]

A more serious problem struck on the second pit stop. Running strong, McElreath pulled into the pits for fuel and tires. The crew, working efficiently, filled the fuel tank and changed the tires in twenty-six seconds, seven seconds faster than the first stop, but as the car pulled away, the engine died. Jack grabbed a borrowed portable starter and inserted it into the rear of the car, but the cable plug fell out of the battery cart. They plugged it in but it fell out again. With sparks flying, pit crewmember Arnold Robinson bravely grabbed the plug and held it in while Jack started the engine. McElreath roared away, but he had lost a critical minute and seven seconds due to the delay.[27]

The car continued to run well but McElreath could not make up the difference lost in the frustrating pit stop. Taking the checkered flag was Graham Hill, who finished a mere fifty seconds ahead of the hard charging Trackburner. Instead of finishing first with a payday of more than $150,000, the Zink car came in third, winning $30,000 and another near miss at the world's most prestigious race. Despite that disappointment, the team rebounded well and McElreath came in second in the Champion series.[28]

The 1967 season started with all eyes on Andy Granatelli's new STP car, powered by a Pratt and Whitney turbine engine, a technology the Zink team had first experimented with almost seven years earlier. Again with Jim McElreath at the wheel, the Trackburner qualified on the fourth row at a speed of 164.241 miles per hour. Having been modified so extensively since acquired from Brabham, the car was entered as a design by Dennie Moore.

The race was not even close until near the end. As one *Tulsa World* reporter stated, the STP car "ran over the world's fastest cars the way Hannibal and his elephants would have crushed an outdoor toilet in the Alps." The powerful new turbine car dominated until lap 197, when its transmission failed. Parnelli Jones, piloting the odd-looking yellow car,

coasted into the pits, only a few short laps from making history. As the year before, McElreath ran well, but due to a malfunctioning part, he took four pit stops instead of the two planned. Most other drivers took only two stops. This time, he came in fifth, three laps behind the winning car driven by A.J. Foyt. [29]

After the race, when he normally would be looking at the coming year already, Jack turned his mind to a different question. Would he mount another assault on Indy? For seventeen years, he and his team members had chased the greatest prize in the world of automobile racing. They had won twice, come close numerous times, and set the curve of technical innovation with the roadsters, the rear-engine Grand Prix-style cars, and the turbine. What more did they have to prove?

There were two other factors weighing on Jack's mind. One was simply

the cost of staying in the lead pack at Indy. In 1952 Jack had run well with a modest investment of $20,000; in 1967 one engine alone cost $20,000, on top of which there was a new chassis every year, spare engines to buy, tires that cost $5,000 a race, and rising costs for full-time crew members. When Urshel and Slick said they had satisfied their urge to put a car on the track, Jack either had to find another financial partner or back the entire effort himself.

More important, however, was the time required to stay at the top. Most financial sponsors were absentee partners, willing to pay the bills and simply come to the races. Jack was not that kind of an owner. Yes, he put up the money, but he also designed cars, developed strategies, managed the team, and tore into engines with grease on his hands. If he could not spare the time to be part of every phase of the experience, he did not

The 1967 season was the last Championship Series for Jack and the John Zink Company Race Team.

want to be involved. And with the expansion of his business, the retirement of his father, and the birth of his first three sons, he did not have time to spare. He made up his mind. If he returned to Indy, it would be as a spectator, not a car owner. After seventeen years setting the pace at the Speedway, Jack was ready for something new.

———⚬⚬⚬———

Stepping away from Indy-style racing did not mean Jack was through with speed. He still craved the thrill of competition and the pursuit of technical perfection, but it had to match the patterns of his changing life. Surprisingly, for a man who had built an international reputation for his mastery of engines, power, and mechanical innovation, Jack found a new passion for speed on the water, and it was not speed boats. It was sailing.

Jack had sailed for the first time in 1963, four years before what turned out to be his last Indy race. He was instantly hooked. Typically, he read all he could about the sport, checked with other enthusiasts, and bought his first boat. In a radical departure from his experience in auto racing, where he always bought the most exclusive, high-priced machinery available, he settled on a modest nineteen-foot Lightning-class sailboat that could be seen on any waterway across the country. It may not have been high tech, but it was perfect for Jack Zink. [30]

The Lightning Class sailboat was designed in 1938 by John and George Barnes, two boat builders in upstate New York who wanted a nineteen-foot craft economical to build, with room for a family and the high level of performance required for a one-design class racer. It had a hard chine, was easy to ramp off and on a trailer, and was fitted with simple rigging that offered sophisticated sail shape controls, including a large spinnaker that allowed the sailor to use strong winds to reach breathtaking speeds. By 1964 there were 11,000 boats registered with the International Lightning Class Sailboat Association. [31]

The Lightning offered Jack the kind of challenge he enjoyed. There was plenty of competition throughout the year, which fit his erratic schedule,

Sailing satisfied Jack's hunger for speed, performance, careful preparation, and a good time with friends. Always frugal, Jack did not like to throw anything away, including this pair of patched-up trouosers.

and each race required a wide range of skills, both technical and tactical, as well as teamwork by a three-person crew. As he told a reporter, "I find it takes demanding concentration and exacting preparation," which reflected both his professional career as an engineer and his second career as a racecar team owner.

For his first race, Jack did not enter a modest local event. Instead, he took on the region's best sailors from Oklahoma, Missouri, Kansas, Nebraska, and Arkansas in the Central States Sailing Association when they held their area championship regatta on Oklahoma's Fort Gibson Lake in June of 1964. Despite his inexperience, Jack's intuitive ability to grasp the important nuances of new avocations served him well. Incredibly, he won the first time out and qualified for the national regatta to be held later that summer in San Diego. As if to prove that was no fluke, he entered a highly competitive race the next weekend on Lake Hefner in Oklahoma City. With experienced sailors Rod and Phyllis Wood as crewmates, he won again. [32]

From 1964 to 1975, Jack and his crewmates won the regional regatta eight times and earned a spot in the national competition. Typical of that experience was his second trip to nationals in 1965, when he competed against 120 boats from across the country. Jack and his crew of Jim Hobson and Rod Wood came in twelfth and fifteenth in the first two qualifying races, and sixth in the finals held on Barnegat Bay off the coast of New Jersey. Over the years, Jack's crew included a wide range of friends and family, especially his son, Colin. The one constant was winning. [33]

Racing sailboats, although satisfying, could not quench Jack's appetite for competition, even with his attention diverted most of the time by his expanding business empire and his second marriage, to Bette Jones, a graduate of the Kansas City Institute of Art, and the birth of their son Darton. Jack needed the smell of the garage, the challenge of technological innovation, and the teamwork that produced results at high speeds. He had walked away from the Indianapolis 500, but Jack could never turn his back on automobile racing. Instead, he turned his attention to modified stockcars on regional tracks.

Jack with his wife, Bette, and sons (left to right) Darton, Colin, Neel, and Whitney.

Jack was always pushing the limits on speed and performance, whether it was on the track, off-road, or on the speed flats where he hoped to break a world record on this bullet-shaped motorcycle (facing page). To his disappointment, it was too unstable to race.

Jack had always liked stockcars. They were the "working man's" kind of racing, affordable, accessible, and personal. He had owned stocks since 1949, when he and Buzz Barton dominated tracks across the state, and he had maintained a stable of stockcars off and on since that time. With his racing team garage at the plant, Jack could tear into an engine or help design a new suspension system and get to the local races in Tulsa, Oklahoma City, Wichita, and other racing venues when possible. Helping make it possible to continue with stockcars was his chief mechanic, Dennie Moore, who had been Jack's partner in racing since 1953. With Dennie building and maintaining cars, Jack could be part of the team despite the increasing demands of business and family on his time.

In 1968, as if to prove they still could get a team to Victory Lane, Jack and Dennie put Buddy Cagle into their green number "52" stock car. Cagle dominated the local track, finishing with twice as many points as the nearest competitor. Still, that was not good enough. Dennie Moore, speaking to the press, said "we had a good car this last year, but we will have an even better one next year." [34]

The new super modified stock car was painted pink and white, long known as "Zink Pink," a nod to the 1955 Indy winning car driven by Bob Sweikert. It had a Chevrolet engine, with a displacement of 304-cubic-inches, a four-barrel Holley carburetor, and a stock ignition system. The cockpit was protected by a cage made of heavy steel tubes, with windows covered by a heavy mesh screen to keep the driver's left arm from flailing outside the car in the event of a rollover. The chassis was a new design, with the engine tilted as in the team's Indy cars, so the driveshaft could run alongside the driver instead of under his seat. This lowered the car's center of gravity, put the driver lower in the cockpit, and cut eighteen inches from the roofline to decrease drag. Weight was reduced another fifty pounds by replacing the complex torsion bar suspension with a single transverse spring. "This is the finest modified racing car I've ever seen," declared Cagle, a veteran driver who had seen hundreds of cars. [35]

For the next four years, Cagle backed up his predictions of greatness by winning both races and championships with regularity. The winning habit continued after 1972, when Jack and Dennie turned the car over to another legendary local driver, Emmett Hahn, who immediately won the Tulsa Speedway Championship and finished first or second every year thereafter until 1980, when Jack suddenly pulled the car from competition. The racing community reacted with surprise. After more than three decades of automotive racing success, everything seemed to be going the right direction for the Zink Racing Team. They had a great car, a great driver, and a chief mechanic with a world-class reputation. And Jack still loved the thrill of speed and the satisfaction of competition. Despite all of this, Jack's life had taken a few surprising turns. Once again, Jack was moving on. [36]

"Moving on" was an apt description of Jack's business career. By the late 1960s the family-owned John Zink Company was expanding more than fifteen percent a year with offices and staff on three continents. A steady stream of new products, especially in pollution control, was coming off the production line, while sales and profits continued to climb. It was inevitable that the world's corporate giants would take notice.

One of the suitors was Sunbeam Corporation, a Chicago-based, diversified manufacturing business known around the world for its small appliances sold under a variety of brand names that included Osterizer and Northern Electric. Sunbeam, with annual sales of more than $450 million, had already branched into other industrial subsidiaries, such as the Illinois Water Treatment Company and Bally Coolers, Inc., and they were looking for additional acquisitions that would complement those enterprises and continue to reduce their dependence on consumer sales. In the fall of 1969, Jack started negotiating with Sunbeam officials. [37]

By December a tentative agreement was announced. The John Zink Company would remain an independent subsidiary of Sunbeam with Jack as President, while John, already retired from day-to-day management, would serve as a consultant. In exchange, the family would receive Sunbeam stock worth more than $29 million, with an escalation clause that could increase that amount depending on profitability over the next two years. The transaction made the Zink family the largest single stockholder of Sunbeam Corporation, with about ten percent of outstanding shares. [38]

Dennie and Jack designed a new super modified stock car (facing page) that dominated tracks in the region.

On February 26, 1972, details of the final deal were unveiled. Sunbeam President R.P. Gwinn, appearing at the Zink Ranch, announced that the marriage of the two firms would be consummated on June 1, 1972, with the Zink family receiving 1,208,447 shares of Sunbeam stock worth $40,634,030. As promised, Jack became a member of the Sunbeam Board of Directors and a member of the Executive Committee. With annual profits of more than $3 million and a staff of almost 600, Jack was determined to grow the company even more. [39]

While contemplating new directions for growth, Jack put additional resources into traditional programs that had served the company for years. One such program was the three-day burner school that had been conducted at the Tulsa plant several times a year since 1950. In 1972 the company hosted six sessions, each with thirty to forty students drawn from all corners of the world. Through a balance of classroom instruction and practical experience at the $3 million research facility, engineers and operations personnel from refineries and chemical plants studied fundamental burner design, fuel characteristics, fuel conservation, heat transfer, and fluid flow. [40]

Offered at no cost, the burner schools served as an effective marketing tool for John Zink products and services, especially as the company pushed more aggressively into international markets. One of Jack's more prominent partners was New Jersey-based Lummus Company, an international firm that designed and constructed petrochemical plants and refineries using burners manufactured by the John Zink Company. In May of 1979, Jack provided the instruction and Lummus paid the travel expenses for representatives from Japan, India, Brazil, and Chile to attend a burner school where they learned about fuel conservation, emergency flares, and burner operating techniques. [41]

While Jack aggressively sought potential customers for traditional burners, the world was beating a path to his company for help in fighting pollution. In 1970 the United States Congress passed an act consolidating fifteen federal pollution programs into one, the new Environmental Protection Agency, with a mandate to clean up America's water, land, and air. It worked. From 1970 to 1980, the annual amount of money spent on pollution reduction and control went from less than $20 billion to more than $60 billion. Similar efforts to reduce pollution were taking place around the world, from Mexico City and Rio to London and Tokyo. The John Zink Company was on the cutting edge of designing and fabricating much of that new technology. [42]

At its basic level, each pollution control device shipped out of a Zink plant was a high-performance burner and "scrubbing system" that treated and reduced waste to a disposable form. The variables were endless, calculated by engineers and applied under controlled conditions at the test furnaces in Tulsa. One reporter, observing the seemingly endless stream of toxic wastes being tested at the plant, found an appropriate metaphor when he wrote, "The conversation-impairing roar among the maze of pipes, dials, and tubing leading from burners located at the front of the plant is the voice of research." Although Jack no longer had the time to oversee every project, he and Gene McGill, the head of the new research division, assigned each case to one engineer, who designed, tested, installed, and tested again every piece of equipment. "It's each engineer's own work and he stands or falls on his own ability," McGill told the reporter. "If we make a mistake, we'll be here next year to fix it." [43]

The emphasis on research and development opened even more doors for the expanding company as the energy industry changed under the pressures of declining domestic production, a greater reliance on oil from the Middle East, and the search for new ways to recover more difficult petroleum deposits. During the 1970s, much of the world's oil was shipped by super tankers. When oil was pumped into the tankers, toxic and potentially explosive vapors were vented into the atmosphere. When oil was pumped out of the tankers, the volatile mixture of fuel and incoming air also created highly flammable vapors.

The John Zink Company developed a "gas-safety" system that produced a non-explosive gas which was pumped into the holds as oil was pumped out, while toxic fumes displaced when oil was pumped in were either safely combusted or gathered, condensed, and recovered. By 1979 all tankers registered in the United States were required to have such a safety system, and non-U.S. tanker fleet owners quickly followed suit. The systems, which could only be tested at the Zink plants in Tulsa, were soon adapted to other operations where oil was pumped from one source to another, including refineries, liquefied petroleum gas terminals, large loading docks, oil tank farms, and gasoline tank truck terminals. [44]

The high cost of foreign oil, especially after the Arab Oil Embargo of 1973, set off a new boom in the search for alternative fuels and a corresponding effort to recover oil and other hydrocarbons in forms which previously were not economical. In the American West, engineers had known for years about rich deposits of shale oil and coal liquids, but they were difficult to extract and even more difficult to process into a product that could be burned efficiently without the release of toxic levels of nitrogen oxides (NOx). Jack and his team at the John Zink Company worked with engineers at Phillips Petroleum Company to solve the latter problem.

Zink's work on low-NOx burners began in 1970 and progressed from research to development and ultimately to a commercial product. The unit was a two-stage combustion burner that controlled the combustion reaction speed of high nitrogen fuels so that very low NOx levels could be achieved in the combustion byproducts. In 1979 officials at the John Zink Company and Phillips Petroleum announced that they had successfully tested a ten-million BTU-per-hour prototype burner. Within two years the unit was on the market at a cost of $25,000, fifty percent more than a traditional burner. [45]

By 1980 the John Zink Company had stretched every measure of success. Profits were up on ever-increasing revenues. The Skiatook plant had doubled in size in 1975. And the international reach of the company was still expanding with plants or offices in England, Italy, Germany, France, and the Netherlands. The company remained the leading firm in industrial burners for the petrochemical industry, and in the growing market of controlling hazardous waste, the John Zink Company had no peer. In a survey conducted by the American Institute of Chemical Engineers, researchers found that there were 119 companies that manufactured liquid-injection incinerators with 219 systems in operation. The John Zink Company had manufactured 75 of those systems, a third of the market share. Despite this success, Jack sensed it was time for another chapter in his life. [46]

A number of changes had occurred during the past fifteen years. He had married Bette and become the father of a fourth son, Darton. His beloved mother, Swannie, had passed away, followed by his father, John, who died in 1973. And although he still enjoyed the research and development challenges of the burner business, he was uncomfortable with the corporate culture

Burners designed, tested, and installed by the John Zink Company could be found in furnaces like these around the world by the 1970s.

and union politics that had followed the merger with Sunbeam.

Jack, like his father, was frugal. Before the merger, if he needed new equipment and he had the cash on hand, he bought it. If he did not, he waited. Like his father, Jack held down overhead expenses, using commercial airlines instead of corporate jets, driving a station wagon instead of a company-owned Mercedes, and decorating his office with racing trophies instead of auction-house art. Such frugality was seen as eccentric in many corporate circles where penthouse executives spent shareholders' money rather than their own.

The other change was Jack's relationship with the workforce. Since working on the floor of the foundry during World War II, Jack had seen himself as one of the boys, ready to do an honest day's work for an honest day's pay. In his mind, he and his workers were peers searching for answers to problems and finding efficiencies in the way they manufactured their products. When the plant unionized in 1970, that camaraderie suffered. Suddenly, on one side was labor and on the other side was management, and although the management was still in Jack's hands, the increasing size of the company combined with the corporate culture of Chicago-based Sunbeam to cast a growing shadow over labor relations. Rulings by the National Labor Relations Board, strikes at the Skiatook plant, and compromises in economy and efficiency gradually wore on Jack.[47]

In 1981 Jack saw a way to make a new start when a take-over attempt was directed at Sunbeam Corporation. It started when IC Industries offered $32 a share for Sunbeam stock, a premium price that far exceeded the value of the stock in 1974 when Jack had sold 150,000 shares at $19 to help settle his father's estate. Jack, his family, and his father's foundation still owned more than a million shares. Then Allegheny International, Inc. entered the fray and offered $41 a share. Jack, over the objections of the other Sunbeam directors and officers, publicly announced that he was going to sell his shares on the open market. On October 31, 1981, Jack completed the transaction. For the first time since 1930, the John Zink Company would be in the hands of someone other than a member of the Zink family. [48]

Once again, it was time to move on.

To generate business and promote the technical prowess of the John Zink Company, Jack (facing page and right) established a burner school that brought engineers and technicians to Tulsa from around the world.

A Sprint to the Finish Line

"Happiness is in the journey, not the destination."

Jack Zink

CHAPTER SIX

As an engineer, Jack Zink understood change. He had mastered the chemical changes in compounds during combustion. He had observed the results of change in automotive technology as bodies became more aerodynamic and engines grew more powerful. He had watched with interest the world around him, as cities spread in all directions and the pace of life quickened under the pressures of social, economic, and technological change. For a curious man who carried a slide rule in his pocket, life was full of fascinating surprises, a constantly evolving and adapting place that offered both challenges and opportunities.

The decade of the 1970s presented Jack with a variety of both. He had expanded his company under the corporate banner of Sunbeam, then decided to sell when the time was right and the price was attractive. He had lost his mother and father, then worked with his family to expand the family foundation for charitable giving. And he had walked away from the stimulating world of open-wheel, Indy-style racing, then found a new type of racing that satisfied his yearning for speed and competition. This time, it was a new breed of racing surprisingly perfect for this middle-aged executive—off-road endurance.

——◦◦◦——

This new passion for speed, unfettered by the confines of pavement, started with motorcycles, which had been a part of Jack's life since he was a teenager driving a 45-cubic-inch Harley and riding in a motorcycle club called the Daredevils. Twenty years later, in the 1960s, a new generation of trail bikes appeared on the market designed by American companies, such as Harley-Davidson and Greeves, and Japanese innovators such as Honda, Yamaha, and Kawasaki. The new bikes were light and rugged, with high clearance and knobby tires perfect for climbing and jumping. Jack quickly bought one of the bikes, a Husqvarna, commonly known as a Husky, and started learning the limits of how hard and fast he could push both himself and his bike over rugged terrain.

Eager to test his skills, Jack staged an enduro event on the Zink Ranch in 1968. The fifty-two-mile timed stage race was limited to motorcycles and organized into four classes: less than 125 cc, 126 to 200 cc, 201 to

After taking his last car to Indianapolis, Jack turned to off-road racing, beginning with motorcycles driven both by himself and others, including this young rider navigating a course at the Zink Ranch.

360 cc, and more than 361 cc. More than 100 riders showed up from three states, but Jack was not one of them. He had broken his foot while trying to ride up a dirt bank. "Don't get the wrong idea about motorcycles," he told a reporter, "they are really quite safe. I was just showing off when this happened." [1]

In the fall of 1972, Jack's passion for motorcycles filled another need. "I noticed I wasn't my usual self," he later told a reporter. "I enjoyed my work but did not seem to have much drive. I knew something was wrong so I talked to my wife about it." The next day he called two friends, Roger Wheeler, president of Telex Corporation, and Vern Street, an engineer with Phillips Petroleum, and asked them if they would join him in a little outing. He wanted to race his motorcycle in the Mexican-1,000, a brutal off-road race down the Baja Peninsula. Accustomed to such suggestions from their competitive friend, they said, "sure." [2]

The plan was for Zink and Street to share the riding. They trained both on and off the bike, gathered fuel and extra parts, and stocked up on precautionary supplies such as antibiotics, water purification pills, pain pills, and sounding devices in case they found themselves lost in the desert. When they got to the starting camp, they were met by more than 300 entrants and thousands of support personnel with vehicles that ranged from motorcycles and dune buggies to cars and trucks.

When the starting gun was fired, Jack bolted from the crowd on his Husky just as the sun was going down. Although he knew himself well enough to know he tended to overdrive his headlights, the adrenaline was flowing and he barreled ahead aggressively despite the growing darkness. As he topped his first steep hill, he found himself airborne when he discovered the trail took a sharp left turn on the other side. "The only consolation was I looked down and saw three or four sets of tire tracks in the cactus and dust, so I knew some others had made the same mistake," he later told a reporter. He recovered and kept going.

The forty-four-year-old executive drove through the night, stopping twice to repair the bike and crashing once to avoid hitting a woman and her child as he drove through a small hamlet. After 525 miles of desert driving, he handed the bike over to his partner who finished the race.

Jack and Dennie built a two-seat dune buggy, which they raced in the Baja 500. This map kept by Jack plotted their course.

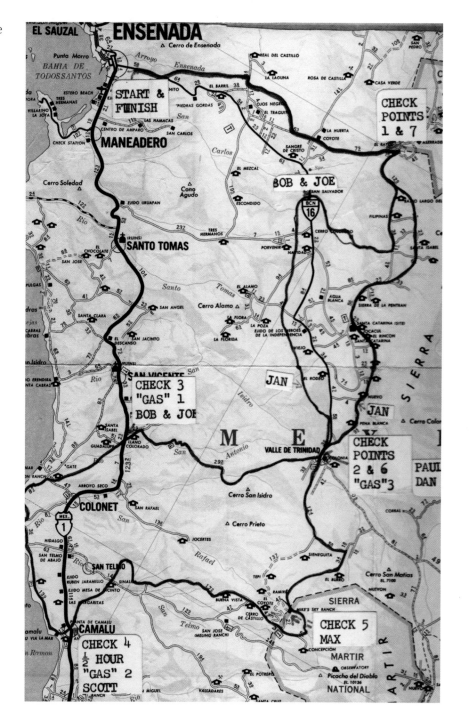

They came in seventh in the motorcycle division, with a time of twenty-five hours, eleven minutes. It did not take long for Jack to start thinking about the next time he would challenge the course and himself once again.[3]

That winter, Jack and Dennie Moore worked on a two-seat dune buggy for the world's biggest off-road race, the Baja 500. Designed by Jack and built by Dennie, it started with a lightweight chassis formed from tubing and powered by a "juiced up" Volkswagen engine with a displacement of 2,200 cc. The sturdy little car was named the ZORR, which stood for Zink Off-Road Racer. "It is designed for endurance," Jack told the press before the race. "We want to make sure it will last for 501 miles."[4]

When asked by a reporter why he was subjecting himself to the danger of such a race, he thought for a moment and spoke from the heart: "I race for many of the same reasons other men whack a golf ball or hunt quail... I find it entertaining and relaxing, but it really goes beyond that. Racing stimulates me...it keeps me mentally alert and forces me to keep in good physical condition. Racing is a great disciplinarian and I sincerely think it helps me do my job better...I'll come back from the Baja refreshed and renewed and a lot more productive." Over the Memorial Day weekend of 1973, when many of their longtime racing friends were headed for Indianapolis, Jack and Dennie climbed into their truck and started driving west.[5]

Their destination was Ensenada, Mexico, the starting point for the Baja 500, which dipped 250 miles into the desert before returning north. The course included dry river beds, gullies, and faint desert trails. "Roads are scarce and the going is torturous," wrote one reporter, with speeds as slow as fifteen miles per hour and as fast as 120 miles per hour. On the day of the race, Jack crawled into the driver's seat with Dennie next to him in the passenger's seat. As rookies, they started in 171st place, which meant they had to eat the dust of those ahead of them and avoid the wrecks and breakdowns that took half of the cars and trucks out of the race.

Everything went well for the first seven hours, but then the rough terrain took its toll when the shock absorber brackets sheared. Despite the rough ride, they kept the pedal down and steadily worked their way through the field. After fifteen hours and forty-nine minutes of driving, the ZORR came across the finish line in third place, forty-eight minutes

Dennie Moore joked that he noticed most of the dents were on his side of the two-seat dune buggy, so he built a one-seater for Jack powered by a Porsche engine (left and facing page).

A SPRINT TO THE FINISH LINE

behind Jack's good friend and winner of the race, Parnelli Jones. Once again, Jack was pleased with the outcome, but knew he could do better. [6]

To prepare for the next race and avoid surprises at 100 miles per hour, Jack and his friend Paul Messick rode motorcycles on a pre-race tour of the course in early June of 1974. Under the brutal conditions, both bikes broke down. On race day, Jack and Dennie were running strong when they topped a rise and found a disabled truck slowly making its way back to the starting line. "We almost missed him," said Jack after the race. They collided, came to a dusty halt, and found that a shock absorber was ripped off and the right rear tire was damaged. They kept going.

After 150 miles of hard driving, the confident Tulsa duo found themselves leading the race by six minutes. "We were passing cars that the experts claimed had a shot at the over-all victory," said Jack. Then the engine started missing. They did a quick check, decided they could break the engine down and fix it, but it would take more than an hour and a half, which would take them out of contention. Jack decided to keep going despite the loss of power. Although they did not place, they finished. To one reporter back home, Jack described the Baja experience as "rugged, romantic and an interesting challenge. We're getting to know our way around...it's not as foreign as it once was." [7]

A year later, Jack's methodical preparation included a pre-race practice run over the course while describing the twists, turns, and obstacles into a tape recorder. His plan was to wear headphones during the real race and listen to his own description of the coming terrain once the race began. Although he thought the extra days in the field would be a good investment of time, he knew the living conditions might take a physical toll on the team. As he told a reporter, "When we get up in the morning, we ask each other how we like our eggs...we say over easy and then we open a package of jerky....In the evening, we ask each other how we want our steaks. Rare. And we open another package of jerky. When we get ready to go to bed, we unroll our sleeping bags and call it the Zink Hilton." [8]

On race day, facing sixty-four competitors in the two-seat division, Jack and Dennie started well but quickly lost power as one cylinder of the VW engine started missing. After continuing on for seventy miles another cylinder started missing. They pulled out for a pit stop and discovered that the bone jarring course had loosened several ignition wires. Dennie

reattached them and they started working their way back to the front of the pack after losing more than seven minutes. "This is the kind of race that doesn't allow you any respite," Jack said later. "You go flat out every mile...it's hard on you physically and psychologically, but that's why you do it... you have to meet the challenge." [9]

Jack made up most of the lost time wherever the course hit sections that twisted and turned sharply. His lightweight buggy may have lacked the power of the big trucks, but his car was nimble and quick. As one reporter noted, "the little Tulsa-built car passed competitors with abandon." About thirty miles from the finish line, when everything seemed to be going well, the car crashed into a foot-long rock and damaged the right rear tire and rim. With a skimpy lead, they decided there was no time for a tire change so they continued running on the thin inner tire. Although it smoked constantly the rest of the way, the backup tire held up and they won the race. After three years, Jack and Dennie were the winning team in their class of the Baja 500. [10]

Each year from 1973 to 1980, Jack and Dennie averaged five to six off-road races across the country, including the Mint 400, the Baja 500, the Cobra 300, the Parker 400, and Sandmaster. Along the way were many adventures. In February of 1975, they were leading the Parker 400 in the deserts of Arizona when the brakes went out. They lost control, vaulted off a low cliff, and hit a telephone pole to put them out of the race. The next year, running the Parker 400 again, Jack was speeding along at 100 miles per hour down a dry river bed when he vaulted off of a 150-foot-tall cliff. The result was two black eyes and a head laceration that took forty stitches to close. "I was trying to run a 400 mile race like a trophy dash," he later lamented. "I was going too fast for the conditions." [11]

Surprises came in all forms. In 1979, during a practice run in the Arizona desert, he was running a rugged stretch of ground at eighty miles per hour when he tried to avoid a rock outcropping and slammed into a rock bluff. The impact caused a rock slide which pummeled Jack and the car. He dug out and walked eight miles through the mountains wearing thin-soled racing shoes. In another mishap during a practice run, his car flew through the air, came down

Before taking on rugged off-road endurance courses, Jack (facing page) would drive the routes before the races with a tape recorder in his lap, dictating notes describing what was around the next turn and over the next rise.

on a rock, and ruptured a fuel line. Jack crawled out of the car and scrambled up a nearby bluff as the car exploded in a ball of flame.[12]

In the Mexicali 500 he came around a bend and almost ran into a stranded driver whose motorcycle had broken down. "I was going through a wash of heavy sand, and if you stopped, you were stuck," Jack recalled. "All of a sudden, out jumped this rider waving his arms. I couldn't stop, but about a quarter of a mile down the road I started to think, I guess I will apply the Golden Rule...so I turned around to go back and get him. When I came by, I slowed down and he jumped on. He rode all the way to the next check point hanging onto the top of my car. It was better than dying in the desert." [13]

Jack prepared for such races as if he was designing a new burner or expanding his company into a new country. For physical conditioning, he designed and built what he dubbed a "Z-tank," two ten-foot metal stock tanks welded together to give him a five-foot deep pool for swimming. He built a harness suspended from above, added a filter and heater set at ninety-four degrees, and calculated how many minutes he needed to swim in place to get the same benefit as swimming 800 yards. For mental conditioning, he regularly raced around the Zink Ranch roads cleared by his father with the ever-active bulldozer. In 1975, as part of the training regimen, Jack staged a series of sanctioned off-road races at the ranch that included the Cobra 200, with fourteen laps, of 14.3 miles each, around a course described by several veteran drivers as "better than the Baja because you don't have cactus." [14]

In 1977 Dennie built a new off-road vehicle for Jack. "I noticed that all the dents and damage on the two-seat ZORR were on my side," Dennie good naturedly recalled years later, "so I built him a one-seater." The new car was powered by a 2,200 cc Porsche engine capable of sustained speeds exceeding 120 miles per hour. It weighed 1,250 pounds and was equipped with special lights that reached far into the desert night. At the age of fifty, when most men were content to ride a lawn mower, Jack was asked by a reporter if he ever felt fear. "It's not really the fear of dying that enters my mind," he responded. "It's the fear of losing." [15]

Once he found his trusty balance of courage and caution, Jack did not

Jack won more than a dozen off-road races, including the Big River 500, the Laughlin 300, the Wet'N'Wild 150, the Parker 400, the Cobra 100, the Cobra 150, and the Baja 500.

lose often. From 1973 to 1980, he won more than a dozen races, including the Big River 500, the Laughlin 300, the Wet 'N Wild 150, the Parker 400, the Cobra 100, the Cobra 150, and the granddaddy of them all, the Baja 500. Parnelli Jones, an Indy-500 winner who was a perennial winner of the Baja 500 in his "fire-breathing Ford Bronco," described Jack this way: "Zink never concedes the possibility that he might not win. He leaves the starting line with the smell of victory in his nostrils." [16]

That same competitive spirit drove Jack to seek another title, and it was not in the world of racing. It was in the unlikely arena of politics.

In 1979 Jack once again needed something new. His company, now a subsidiary of Sunbeam, had become an international, diversified industrial giant with department managers, organized labor unions, and corporate policies. He had seen the company through its infancy and development phases, which required his personal energy at every turn, but now it was a structured behemoth that wanted him only at arm's length, dealing with corporate issues, propping up stock prices, and leading the pack in long term planning. He missed the daily stimulation of working in the test furnaces, finding solutions to real and immediate problems. On top of that, he found himself in a bitter controversy with the top officials of Sunbeam. When a hostile takeover effort bumped the price of Sunbeam stock to previously high levels, Jack, as one of the largest stockholders in the company, thought they should sell and take the profits. His fellow board members disagreed. While the issue dragged on in public toward its ultimate conclusion and sale, Jack gradually backed out of his top management positions at the John Zink Company. The firm his father had founded and the company he had grown to international prominence would soon be managed for the first time by someone other than a member of the Zink family.

At loose ends, Jack found the challenge he craved when he read that his friend, United States Senator Henry Bellmon, would not seek reelection for another term. In March of 1979, Jack told a reporter that he was "looking at running for the Republican nomination." Although he had always voted,

In 1979 Jack took on yet another new kind of race, when he ran for the United States Senate seat vacated by his friend, Henry Bellmon.

he had never immersed himself in politics, either at the party level or with individual candidates. He liked the prospect of the competition, but more important was a sense that he had something to offer, a belief that he could make a difference. "The United States is a big business with tens of thousands of subsidiaries," Jack said. "We have to develop incentives for the investment of capital for manufacturing capability...we have allowed the erosion of our productivity and we need to turn that around. I know how to run a business." Asked to describe himself within the party spectrum, Jack placed himself "somewhere between Ronald Reagan and Charles Percy." In August of 1979, Jack formally announced he would seek the nomination of his party in the coming primary. [17]

With the election still a year in the future, Jack organized the venture as he would a campaign to build a new racecar or design a new burner. First, he assembled his team, led by longtime friend, Ed Spilman, and political activist, Nancy Apgar. Spilman was an experienced sports journalist who had been one of the first reporters to cover the young Jack Zink and his racing exploits in the late 1940s and early 1950s. Ed had traveled extensively with the race team and had even served on Jack's pit crew at the Indianapolis 500. Nancy had experience in a number of political campaigns and would remain a fixture in the Republican Party for many years. [18]

While the Zink political team organized fund-raising efforts and set up speaking engagements, they used their experience with the press to define Jack's message. Most of his policy statements fell into three categories—the economy, energy resources, and foreign policy. Jack quickly came out swinging on the latter. In a speech delivered to the East Tulsa Sertoma Club on October 3, 1979, he attacked President Jimmy Carter's stand on Russian troops stationed in Cuba. "It's bad enough that our power and prestige are being eroded in Europe, the Middle East and the Far East," he said, "but it is disastrous when it happens in the Western Hemisphere." Jimmy Carter, in his opinion, was "encouraging the world to chip away at America's security."

Jack hammered away at the need for a strong defense. "The United States will never see world peace without military superiority," he told a

Jack enjoyed the year-long campaign for the Senate seat. He thrived on the organizational challenges and met many new friends in all parts of the state. One of his most supportive partners in the race was his wife, Bette (below on right).

crowd. He declared that the B-52 bomber was obsolete and the country needed a new bomber, neutron weapons, and the M1-X tank. Voters would not have to guess where he stood on important issues. "The proposed SALT II treaty," he said, "is a farce." [19]

On October 15, 1979, Jack raised the issue of a "Western Hemisphere Energy Alliance." Speaking at the World Business Conference in Madrid, Spain, he suggested that the best defense against the economic assaults of OPEC and the Middle Eastern oil sheiks was a new era of cooperation between the United States, Canada, and Mexico, whose combined known reserves in oil, gas, coal, shale oil, and heavy oil were enough to supply the energy needs of the country for 300 years. "We need to pool petroleum technology and resources with the three countries to achieve independence from Middle East energy brokers," he said. Editorial writers at the *Tulsa World* agreed, publicly stating that "the idea is realistic and one that is almost certain to come about in some form." [20]

Addressing public concerns over rising energy prices and a faltering economy, Jack attacked President Carter's oil import fee. "If not repealed by Congress, the oil import fee would have cost consumers about $12 billion per year and saved only 50,000 to 100,000 barrels of oil a day," he said. "That same money, invested in proper heat conservation apparatus would save two to three times that much energy at a one time cost." Speaking plainly, Jack told one audience that "we need someone who understands the real world. Those people in Washington are living in a fairy world." [21]

As the campaign progressed, Jack articulated a moderate domestic agenda that ranged from agricultural policy to opportunities in the workplace. Reaching out to rural voters, he advocated policies that would protect family farmers. "I think we are going to have to be careful or we are going to eliminate the farm family in one generation," he told a crowd in Western Oklahoma. "I think we ought to eliminate inheritance taxes on farmland so they can pass it on to their children." Speaking to the conservative Eagle Forum, he defended his stand on equal opportunities for women. Although he opposed the Equal Rights Amendment, Jack said the country needed to protect equal opportunities for both sexes in the workplace. As for the divisive issue of abortion, he said he was against abortion, but he did not believe abortion needed to be addressed by the federal government or in a constitutional amendment. [22]

Jack took advantage of his reputation as a successful businessman, especially when he focused his message on the economy and the inflationary spiral that had started during the Vietnam War. Speaking directly to his potential opponents in the campaign, he issued a challenge: "Everyone wants to do the right thing...the question is how to do it. Do you have the experience to propose a program?" Jack's economic plan, based on his long experience on the battlefields of business, centered on investment and productivity. "Give the American worker more and better tools to do his job and he will cure this country's inflation-depression tug of war," he said. "If we can increase our productivity just a few percentage points without increasing costs, we will return to a stable economy."

To accomplish this, Jack proposed tax incentives for improved plants and machinery instead of cuts in capital gains, which he said "reward the speculators and money shufflers." He also wanted tax-free, low interest bonds to modernize production plants and a more gradual approach to environmental protection, which was often detrimental to production. "If America is a giant company, then its business is to provide a better life for Americans," he said, "but it can't do that unless we return to sound business principles and spend our money on the things we know will produce that better life." [23]

Jack quickly earned the support of prominent businessmen throughout the state. In November of 1979, he announced that seven Tulsa industrial leaders would serve in a campaign advisory capacity. The group included John Williams, retired chairman of the Williams Companies; John E. Rooney, real estate developer; Robert J. LaFortune, oilman and former mayor; James M. Hewgley, oilman and former mayor; Walter Helmerich III, president of Helmerich and Payne Drilling; E.R. Albert, Jr., chairman of Albert Equipment Co.; and Robert W. Langholz, attorney. Other businessmen from across the state throwing their support to Jack included oilmen Douglas and H.H. Champlin from Enid, banker George Records from Oklahoma City, and oilmen Dick Sias and Edward Joullian III from Oklahoma City. They were joined on the front lines by many Republican Party loyalists such as Joe Coleman, a key player in the state presidential campaign for Ronald Reagan, and Tom Thornbrugh, the former Tulsa County Republican chairman. [24]

As with most political campaigns, Jack's run for the Senate became a family affair, with both support and tolerance coming from wife, Bette, and their eight-year-old son, Darton. From Christmas of 1979 to March of 1980, Jack was on the road two to three days a week, and then the schedule moved into high gear with week-long swings through the state from Little Dixie in the southeast to the Panhandle 250 miles due northwest. "He has more endurance that I do," Bette told a reporter during the campaign. "I can go for about two days at a time, then I need to take a break." [25]

Bette attended campaign events where she could make a contribution. "I try to go to all the coffees and to the Republican Women's clubs where he speaks," she told a reporter. "If there is a red check mark by my name on the schedule, I know I will be going along." Such events included the Strawberry Festival, the Rooster Festival, the Peach Festival, the Watermelon Festival, and one of the biggest parades in the state, 89ers Day in Guthrie, where she rode her horse George, and Darton rode his horse Tommy Cottontail. "Jack is really kind of a fun candidate," she said. "He's a winner. And he's frugal. The meanest thing I ever heard anyone say about him is that he's tighter than the bark on a tree." [26]

Jack adjusted well to the campaign grind. "I've enjoyed the campaign as much as anything I have ever done," he said in an interview while taking a break from what he called "glad handing" at the Flint Steel Company plant. "The toughest thing has been going from a listener to a talker...I've always thought a good executive had to be a good listener...when you're not listening you're not learning. Now, people expect me to do all the talking." He also kept his sense of humor. Telling the reporter about his schedule of starting each day at 4:45 a.m. and not getting to bed until well past midnight, he said he was "living a life of purity." [27]

By July, only a month before the primary election, a poll indicated that the Republican race was down to three front runners with more than half of the registered voters still undecided. Jack had a slight lead, followed closely by thirty-one-year-old State Senator Don Nickles from Ponca City and conservative businessman, Ed Noble, from Tulsa. While the poll showed that Jack's strongest support was centered in the two metropolitan areas and among blue collar workers, Nickles' support came from rural Oklahomans, suburban housewives, and the emerging might of the Moral Majority, a right-wing, Christian-based organization led by the Reverend Jerry Falwell. Noble's support was more limited, although he did gain the endorsement of Citizens for the Republic, a conservative political action committee founded by then-California Governor, Ronald Reagan. [28]

As the primary vote approached, the campaign rhetoric intensified as the trailing candidates focused their attention on the front runner. Noble attacked Jack when he did not appear at a televised debate, which Jack later admitted was a mistake. More damaging was a Moral Majority effort to smear Jack as an "atheist" in fundamentalist churches on the Sunday before the election. Anticipating that tactic, Jack thought he had a chance to offer his stand on religion when he received an invitation to appear on Christian radio station KQCV in Oklahoma City. He never got the chance because, ironically, the radio host steered all questions away from religion. "I was hoping I would be able to explain that I believe religion to be a very personal thing," he told a reporter after the program. "I don't run around trying to push my beliefs off on anybody." [29]

On the eve of the election, the editorial page of the *Tulsa World* strongly endorsed Jack's candidacy: "Zink is the standout in a Republican primary field of five candidates...he is a tireless executive accustomed to problem solving and working with people. His outstanding record is the result of setting goals and organizing people and resources to achieve them, a quality that will serve him well in the U.S. Senate." The editorial writer compared Jack to Henry Bellmon, who "combined a common touch and uncommon ability to win three statewide races...and showed intelligence, a willingness to work long hours, and a knack for getting along with senators in both parties." In the opinion of the editorial writer, Jack was the "obvious choice for the GOP nomination." [30]

On August 26, 1980, voters went to the polls to cast their ballots. That evening at the watch party, Jack, Bette, Darton, and a large gathering of friends watched the television coverage as results came in. For a while he was ahead, then the vote for Nickles picked up and the lead shifted back and forth. As the night wore on it was apparent that neither would gain a majority and that a runoff would be necessary. The next day, when all votes were counted, Nickles led with 47,879 votes to 45,914 votes for Jack. It was essentially a dead heat. [31]

Jack approached the runoff as he would the final laps of the Indianapolis 500. He described his position as "almost in the lead...I can't work any harder, but I can work smarter and I will." In what he called a "beef up," Jack hired forty-year-old Mike McCarville as the new campaign manager and added veteran political worker Mary Ellen Miller, who was nationally known for identifying potential voters. Jack and his staff admitted they had made mistakes in the primary. For the runoff, they would be more aggressive in pointing out differences in the candidates, plus they would pay more attention to getting their committed voters out on election day. "That is where the Zink campaign broke down in the primary," said McCarville. [32]

Despite the changes and the redoubled efforts of family and friends, the final results were no better. Nickles won the runoff and the chance to face the winner of the Democratic primary, Andrew Coats. Jack watched the early returns in Oklahoma City, then flew to Tulsa where he was greeted by a large but subdued crowd. Faced with defeat, he held his head high, smiled, and told his friends and supporters that his first venture into politics was a rewarding experience. "How many people at the age of fifty-two have the chance to gain so many new friends," he said, "while most people my age are trying to hold onto the ones they have." Showing the disappointment, he lamented that he "had a tremendous opportunity to work for the folks...I made the offer and it wasn't accepted." After a full year of shaking hands, life on the road, and the unnatural task of selling himself, it was time to focus once again on the priorities in his life—business, family, the Zink Ranch, and service to the community. [33]

―◦◦◦―

The end of the election campaign, coupled with his exit from the John Zink Company, served as a clean break for Jack as he approached his fifty-third birthday. It did not take long for new doors to open. In 1979 he had purchased a small company called "Product Manufacturing" that made parts for McDonnell-Douglas Aviation and a few components for the energy industry. In 1983, after abiding by a two-year non-competition clause in his exit from the John Zink Company, Jack changed the name from "Product Manufacturing" to Zinkco and returned his focus to what he knew best, combustion equipment for the oil and gas industry. [34]

When the new owners of the John Zink Company complained that the

Upon later reflection, Jack (right) considered his defeat in the Senate race a lucky break. He never again considered an elected office, but remained close to public leaders.

TO INDY AND BEYOND: THE LIFE OF RACING LEGEND JACK ZINK

name "Zink" was an international trademark for combustion equipment in the same way that "Kleenex" was a trademark for tissue and "Xerox" was a trademark for photocopiers, Jack changed the name of his company to Zeeco. He rented space for the company for several months, then built a 20,000 square-foot factory on a 200-acre tract of land in Broken Arrow, a suburb to the southeast of Tulsa. Always ready for a challenge, he was intent on building a world-class research and test facility for the production of burners, flares, and incinerators along with the new company. [35]

Starting small, the company grew slowly at first, paced by Jack's insistence that growth had to be financed through profits, not crippling debt. That policy paid off when the oil and gas industry crashed in the early 1980s following the deregulation of natural gas. Almost a third of all banks in Oklahoma failed, including the nationally infamous failure of Penn Square Bank in Oklahoma City in 1982 and the unprecedented failure of the state's largest bank, First National Bank of Oklahoma City, in 1985. While other firms in the energy industry contracted or closed their doors, Zeeco continued its steady rise from a solid foundation with no debt.

By 1987 Jack described the young company as "state of the art." As he had done thirty-six years before, he nurtured growth through increased market share and technical innovation. "You can't go from step one to step three without going through step two," he told a reporter. "And we're the ones who know how to get to step four." He returned to the field, anywhere combustion equipment was needed, and found applications for his personal brand of service and solutions. He also started building a team, including Dave Surbey, a hard-working and fiercely independent man who could do a little bit of everything. Like Jack, Dave was as comfortable in the board room as he was on the factory floor testing a new piece of equipment. In 1990, Jack appointed Dave president and chief operating officer of Zeeco. [36]

The company's staff grew during the decade of the 1990s, including the addition of a young man who had entered Oklahoma State University's School of Engineering, but graduated instead with a degree in accounting. This new graduate had grown up around combustion equipment in his

Here (facing page), with his third wife Janet, Jack is shown with U.S. Speaker of the House Newt Gingrich (left) and Oklahoma Congressman Steve Largent (right).

After the Senate race and his departure from the John Zink Company, Jack returned to the design, testing, and installation of combustion equipment around the world. His new company was called Zeeco.

TO INDY AND BEYOND: THE LIFE OF RACING LEGEND JACK ZINK

father's company, just as Jack had done almost fifty years earlier. Like Jack, he had assembled parts, met with clients, and tested equipment in the growing number of test furnaces at the plant. Perhaps this was no surprise, because the budding young businessman was Jack's youngest son, Darton, who by now had earned his father's trust.

Jack and his youngest son had always been close. Darton fondly recalled that after going through the normal senior job interviewing process through Oklahoma State's placement office, "Dad matched my lowest offer." When Darton observed that several of his friends had plans to take a few weeks after graduation to travel and see some of the world, Jack replied that it was fine with him, "as long as you are at work at Zeeco on Monday morning." Darton started work in Zeeco's Research/Development and Test Facility, was a sales manager, and then after a few years became controller and later vice president.

In 2000, at the young age of fifty-three, Dave Surbey died unexpectedly of natural causes while on a business trip to India. Darton recalled telling his father, "Dad, with Dave having passed away, I expect you will be here tomorrow to address the employees, tell them what has happened, and explain how we are going to move forward." Jack's reply? "I have no intention of addressing your employees. I have full confidence in you, and in fact, I do not think I am even going to be in the office tomorrow. I expect you to handle it." At the age of twenty-eight, Darton was president of a young company on the cusp of expansion. [37]

Jack, Dave, and Darton had built the company on the back of innovation. In Scotland, they were asked to design a flare in a neighborhood where the codes prohibited both noise and the sight of equipment from the road. Normally, the way to reduce noise from a flare was to build a tall tower that simply directed the noise up and over people on the ground. In this case, a tower was not allowed. The solution was an innovative new type of ground level flare, with operating temperatures as high as 1,800 degrees, surrounded by a heavy heat and sound insulated enclosure. No smoke, no noise...problem solved. [38]

Another challenge came from halfway around the world in Jamnagar, India. Bechtel, an international construction firm, was building a refinery

Zeeco's Free Jet Burner (facing page) is one of the lowest-emission industrial burners in the world.

for Reliance Petroleum that covered four square miles and refined 550,000 barrels of oil a day. For safety reasons, they needed the world's highest capacity flare that could handle a "doomsday scenario" of flaring huge capacities of hydrocarbon gas at a rate of eight million pounds per hour in an emergency. The engineers at Zeeco designed the flare and lifted it into place atop a state of the art, de-mountable stack system and support tower that soared 500 feet in the air. When completed, it was the largest piece of equipment of its kind in the largest grass roots refinery in the world. [39]

Darton continued many of the traditions started by his grandfather in 1930 and expanded upon by his father beginning in 1951. Recalling the challenge before him as the new century approached, Darton said, "In our competitive industry, we had to either grow bigger or get smaller...there was no in between." They grew bigger. Expanding industrial capability at their 200-acre site, Darton and Jack turned Zeeco into a full-service, high-performing company with a full range of products and services that once again included burners, flares, and incinerators.

Leading the way was the Zeeco research and testing facility, which grew to include thirteen full-scale test furnaces that could test virtually any fuel composition and simulate the actual operating conditions to which the equipment would be subjected in refineries or petrochemical plants. Three of the furnaces could fire more than seven burners at the same time, blending fuel gases such as natural gas, hydrogen, propane, nitrogen, carbon dioxide, propylene, butene, butane, and pentane, or liquids such as light oil, heavy oil, naphtha, gasoline, and kerosene. The research and development investments paid dividends. From 1997 to 2004, the engineers at Zeeco received a total of eight patents, roughly one each year. And in the Zink family tradition, the company had no long-term debt. [40]

Building a new company was a great outlet for Jack's undiminished energy after his disappointing loss in the Senate race and departure from the John Zink Company. But unlike the 1950s and 1960s, when he regularly spent twelve hours a day at the plant or on the road, Jack allocated time in his new daily schedule for other pursuits and relied more on

No task was too big for Zeeco, including this huge acid gas incinerator (page 166), one of the largest of its kind in the world.

Zeeco quickly established a reputation for innovative designs and problem solving. Here (page 167), a new flare is prepared for installation at a plant in the Middle East.

TO INDY AND BEYOND: THE LIFE OF RACING LEGEND JACK ZINK

HILLCREST
MEDICAL
CENTER

EAST
ENTRANCE

DEDICATED TO SERVING
THE COMMUNITY,
FAMILIES AND
INDIVIDUALS BY
PROVIDING MODERN
HEALTH SERVICES WITH
HUMAN UNDERSTANDING

Dave Surbey, followed by Darton, to fight the day-to-day battles in the trenches. Later, Jack would say that building the new company from scratch was one of his proudest accomplishments. "I never worked with a finer, more hard working group of individuals than the folks at Zeeco."

At the same time, other than a few motorcycle and bicycle races, Jack pulled back from his passion for racing, which had provided needed relief from the pressures of business for more than thirty years as he progressed from stockcars and midgets to championship cars and off-road dune buggies. The challenge of winning every race was replaced by the challenge of making a difference in the world around him. Denied the privilege of serving all Oklahomans through the office of United States Senator, he was determined to serve the community nonetheless. And just as doors had opened in the world of business, he found welcome arms in the world of community service.

In the early 1960s a reporter searched for keys that explained the phenomenal success of the John Zink Company. As he interviewed Jack, they discussed the usual topics, such as research and development, innovation, a motivated workforce, international expansion, the absence of debt, and service to his customers. But in this one interview, Jack offered another perspective on his own role in the company's expansion. It was his belief in "undiluted interests." As he told the reporter, he focused all of his energies on winning two battles. One was building his business. The other was winning races, whether it was on a track, on the water, or in the desert. He avoided serving on boards of directors, he said, limited his fund-raising responsibilities to writing checks, and refused appointments to committees and commissions at the local, state, and national levels. [41]

During the 1970s, after the John Zink Company became part of the Sunbeam Corporation, Jack made a few exceptions to this general rule. He had accepted one invitation to serve on the Hillcrest Medical Center Board of Directors in 1969. He also served as emcee for the "Symphony Ball," a fundraiser for the Tulsa Philharmonic, in 1977. But in most cases, Jack's

As Dave Surbey and Darton took on increasing leadership roles at Zeeco, Jack had more time for philanthropic work (left) and keeping fit with friends (facing page).

contributions to non-profit organizations came in the form of cash, access to the Zink Ranch, or use of his race cars to draw a crowd. His "undiluted interests" were business and racing. [42]

In 1981 that standing policy was challenged when Jack was approached by city leaders who needed help cleaning up the Tulsa State Fair. In 1970 Tulsa County commissioners had created the Tulsa County Fairgrounds Trust Authority to manage the 240-acre Expo Square at 21st and Yale. There were physical problems with aging structures, some of which dated to the 1920s, as well as highly publicized structural problems with the Expo Building, a modern structure that covered ten acres with a free-span roof supported by high tension cables attached to underground piers. In 1980 county commissioners approved a $1 million line of credit to get the problems fixed, but a year later little work had been done. [43]

The fair also suffered from internal strife. A reporter with the *Tulsa World* described the problems in a feature story: "Political infighting over the fairground and deteriorating public confidence have for the past five years hamstrung any progress towards allowing one of the community's most valuable assets from flowering to its potential." The Trust, according to the reporter, was split into two factions, one supporting and the other advocating the replacement of the "controversial executive director," John Elsner. Once a crown jewel of the community and the site of the famed International Petroleum Exposition, the fairgrounds was in trouble. [44]

Jack, surprising his family and friends, seemed interested. On one side was the challenge, which always appealed to the competitor in him. As the reporter covering the Fair's problems noted, "Zink knows a challenge when he sees one, and he has never learned to resist them." On the other was personal history with the fairgrounds. During the 1930s Jack regularly attended races at the fairgrounds speedway and later became one of the most popular and successful team owners and drivers on the track. He even spent one year managing the speedway. During World War II he rode his horse with the Tulsa Mounted Patrol, which performed during rodeos. And his wife, Bette, had shown horses at the Tulsa State Fair. "I probably have as much appreciation for the broad spectrum of people who use the fairgrounds as anybody," he told the reporter. [45]

In April of 1981, Jack was appointed to the Trust and a year later was named chairman. Expressing his usual optimism, Jack summed up the

challenge with one of his favorite sayings, "A winner says 'I'm good, but not as good as I ought to be'…a loser says 'I'm not as bad as a lot of other people.'" To raise expectations, Jack stressed the assets of the fairgrounds. "Last year the Tulsa Convention Center had 800,000 attendees and the Performing Arts center had 220,000…the Fairgrounds had 3.5 million… this is the most cost effective public facility in Oklahoma, maybe the United States," he said. "It's such a remarkable facility that few people recognize it for its true value."[46]

Jack knew that credibility was essential for a public operation, so he and the board drafted and approved a policy requiring disclosure of even "apparent" conflicts of interest either on the board or on the staff. He changed the accounting of income, expenses, and depreciation of assets to correct the perception that the fair was a money-making operation. He endorsed a number of cost-cutting measures and fee increases to balance the budget. And he pushed through reforms in the way the employees handled cash and ticket receipts. According to one public report, staff members said that Jack arrived at the fair offices almost every day to assign tasks and collect information that could be passed on to the trustees as they considered changes to the operations. A reporter close to the scene wrote that "Zink has done more than bubble with optimism…in his month-long tenure he has guided the board through several decisions that appear to have set the stage for progress."[47]

Coming from the business community, Jack understood the value of concrete, simple goals that would resonate with his customers, in this case the people of Tulsa. "I'm going to eliminate any indication, any area, where a fella could even think something's wrong," he said. "I want to make this baby Simon pure." Jack's second clear goal also came from the business community, where he often said, "we can get bigger or we can get smaller…we can't stay the same." In order to grow the fairgrounds, Jack proposed a combination of public and corporate funding. "The fairgrounds touches every company in this community," he said. "I think they will participate with private contributions."[48]

After years of conflict, the Tulsa Fairgrounds was back on the road to

Jack's many commitments to serving non-profits included stints as chairman of the board of the Tulsa State Fair (left), a significant gift to the Tulsa River Parks System (facing page above), and the Boy Scouts of America (facing page below).

fulfilling its mission to the community. Jack would remain on the Fairgrounds Trust Authority for a few more years, after which he and others organized a 501(c)3 tax-exempt group to keep the momentum going. As recently as 2004, the Friends of the Fairgrounds Foundation, Inc. raised $135,000 for landscaping, renovation of older buildings, and the expansion of programs that drew people to Expo Square. As Jack often said, "sometimes it is the small voice that causes people to think that a good deal is a deal that is good for everyone." To him, the fairgrounds was for everyone.

For the next decade, Jack responded to a long list of requests for his unique brand of service. In the world of business, he was asked to sit on the boards of several corporations, including Telex, Utica National Bank, and Unit Drilling and Exploration Company. The latter was owned by King Kirchner, who had met Jack while the two of them were enrolled at Oklahoma A&M in the late 1940s. As teenagers they shared a passion for motorcycles, lost contact after graduation, but renewed their friendship riding in motorcycle races from the late 1960s to the mid-1970s. King, a native of Perry who had built a small cable tool drilling firm into one of the region's biggest companies, asked Jack to serve on his board of directors in 1982. [49]

"Jack was a great board member," King recalled years later. When King decided to take his company public, Jack helped recruit outside board members such as John Williams of the Williams Companies to lend credibility to the leadership team. Jack also added his balance of caution and courage to the corporate decision-making process. In the mid-1980s, when most drilling firms were either putting their rigs in storage or going out of business, some board members recommended selling the drilling side of the company and sinking all assets into the oil production and marketing division. Jack urged caution, citing the realities of long-term viability. As he pointed out, investors on Wall Street typically priced the stock of oil companies at four to six times the value of total assets, while drilling companies were worth twelve to fifteen times the value of assets. There might be short-term benefits to selling the rigs, but in the long term, they would be better served by limiting debt, holding on to their assets, and waiting for better times in the oil patch. [50] Time validated Jack's advice.

Another long-time acquaintance, David Morgan, sought Jack's experience with both business and automobiles. David, like Jack, was a race car veteran who had raced professionally since 1958. Running under the

banner of Sunray DX, he drove Corvettes on the road racing circuit but ventured into Sebring-style cars, street rods, and dragsters. In 1968 he and his partner, Jerry Grant, won the Daytona Road Race. After walking away from the world of race cars, David asked Jack to help him acquire a Volkswagen dealership. [51]

The two friends drove to San Antonio to talk to Volkswagen's American import distributors. Arriving with impressive balance sheets with both assets and experience, Jack and David confidently answered a series of questions. "Do you know anything about cars?" the distributor asked. "Everything," they said. "Do you know anything about retail sales?" he asked. "Nothing," they said. During their closing statements, Jack may have sensed they were in trouble when he added one last comment, "We're a hell of a lot of fun to do business with." Despite the bravado, they did not get the dealership. [52]

Jack's willingness to help others extended well beyond friends to include the entire community of Tulsa. After his father died in 1973, Jack, his sister Jill, and other members of the family used the John Steele Zink

Foundation to improve the quality of life in their hometown. The list of institutional recipients through the years would span the worlds of health care, the arts, museums, education, and service organizations such as the Salvation Army, Goodwill Industries, Boy Scouts of America, Girl Scouts of the USA, and the National Conference of Christians and Jews. By 2001 the John Steele Zink Foundation was one of the twenty largest foundations in the state with more than $40 million in assets and gifts exceeding $2.5 million each year. [53]

One of the largest gifts ever given by the foundation went to the River Parks Project in Tulsa, an initiative that was especially near and dear to Jack's interests in outdoor recreation, conservation, and youth. In the 1970s officials in Tulsa adopted an ambitious plan to improve land on both sides of the Arkansas River, which wound its way through the heart of the city on its course from the Rocky Mountains to the Mississippi River. Plans included picnic areas, public art, and paved trails for walkers, runners, and bicycle riders. The only problem was the river itself, which seasonally varied from a raging giant filled bank to bank with rushing water, to a mere trickle that exposed nearly the entire river bed—almost a quarter of a mile in width—of unsightly mud and sand. To make the river parks plan work, they needed to control the water with a costly dam.

The Zink family stepped forward to help. With the resources of the John Steele Zink Foundation behind them, they pledged $1 million toward the cost of a low-water dam, if others would step forward as well. They did. The resulting dam created a lake ensuring a more or less constant water level from downtown Tulsa to the dam's location at 31st Street. When the dam was completed and the lake was dedicated, the Tulsa City Council named the body of water Zink Lake. On September 3, 1983, more than 150,000 people joined city leaders and celebrities as they said thanks to Jack, Jill, and the entire Zink family for their legacy of giving back to the community. [54]

Jack's commitment to outdoor recreation had always been strong, but his passion for open spaces and public accessibility became a dominant theme in his life during the 1980s and 1990s. He carved enough time out of his schedule to serve several terms on the River Parks Authority Board,

Jack considered the Zink Ranch one of his family's most important legacies. Foremost among his favorite groups to use the Ranch were Cub Scouts (left) and Boy Scouts (facing page).

where he advocated trails for hiking, biking, and running. In 1989 he accepted an appointment to serve on the Oklahoma Department of Wildlife Commission, where he consistently supported the staff in its efforts to operate more efficiently for the benefit of outdoor recreation. And he was elected to three terms as president of the Indian Nations Council of Boy Scouts, a position he used to advocate outdoor activities for boys, girls, and their parents. The common thread that connected all of these activities was one of the greatest passions of his life, the Zink Ranch.

For almost thirty years, from 1946 to 1973, Jack's father John had built the Zink Ranch into what he called a "poor man's country club." It was close enough to Tulsa to be easily accessible for both the family and their friends, while the 12,000 acres of rolling hills, wooded valleys, and open prairie in southern Osage County offered endless opportunities for hunting, fishing, and any activity that required space. Jack shared his father's passion for the land. He recognized that the Ranch was perfect for his lifelong interests in fitness, teamwork, and the lessons of balancing caution and courage. And he saw the way that individuals and groups used the Ranch to enjoy a brief respite from life in the city. As the years passed, Jack came to realize that the Zink Ranch was an important part of his community's future.

From 1973 to 2004, Jack built the Zink Ranch into a combination of wildlife preserve, outdoor park, and ever-changing venue for activities as diverse as motorcycle races and bird watching. He tripled the size of the ranch to 33,000 acres, adding a few acres one year and entire ranches in others. When his father's original lodge was threatened by the planned flooding which created Skiatook Lake in 1980, Jack built a new lodge farther south on the Ranch. Included were modern living quarters and a museum gallery where he displayed the story of Zink racing through photographs, artifacts, and restored racecars. At the heart of this growing facility was the great hall, a perfect place for banquets and parties where an endless list of groups could raise money for good causes or simply come together to celebrate their common interests.

The Zink Ranch rightfully earned a reputation that spanned the nation. One of the oldest features at the Ranch was the Red Castle Gun Club, with

Jack liked to have fun, whether it was hunting or fishing (left) or a long bike ride with his son, Darton (facing page left).

thousands of members and facilities that regularly won national awards for quality and accessibility. Equally impressive to outside observers was Cub World, a family scouting complex with themed areas called "The Land Ship," "The Native American Nature Center," "Turkey Creek Village," and "King Arthur's Castles." In his dedication to scouting, Jack built the Zink Aquatics Sports Center along the Zink Ranch's shoreline on Skiatook Lake so kids could experience the thrill of sailing and lake activities. To encourage the mothers of Scouts to join their children in campouts, he built lodges and cabins with amenities such as kitchens, fully-equipped bathrooms including showers, and dormitory-style sleeping quarters.

All of these improvements to the infrastructure, combined with the diversity of the terrain and groundcover, attracted a wide range of special events to the Zink Ranch spanning the full spectrum from very loud to very quiet. On the quiet side were groups such as the Audubon Society and the Astronomy Club of Tulsa, which regularly staged events to observe the wonders of nature. Just as quiet were orienteering competitions, in which participants navigated from start to finish using only a map and compass, making observations along the way to evidence their completion of the course. A University of Tulsa orienteering group, in the fall of 2004, described the Zink Ranch course this way: "The property is a peninsula of land surrounded by Skiatook Lake, with cliff faces and boulder fields parallel to the shoreline. Forest covers nearly the entire area, save for the access road and a few outbuildings, most of which is runnable. The northern part of the property contains few distinct features, making the orange course a challenging test of navigational skills."

This combination of rugged beauty and diversity attracted groups of horsemen and women. In the spring of 2004, the Indian Territory Competitive Trail Ride was staged over two days. Their website added to the pastoral image surrounding the reputation of the Zink Ranch: "The terrain consists of lakes and streams, sandy trails, rocky trails through woods, meadows, up and down hills…see wildlife, wild flowers, and beautiful views." Another group invited to use this natural wonderland included the Tulsa Chapter of Women in the Outdoors, which staged an "Outdoor

During the last years of his life, Jack enjoyed an active social and recreational life with his fourth wife, Jan (left above), and friends such as John Groendyke (left), Roy Clark (to right of Jack), and Dale Robertson (at head of table).

TO INDY AND BEYOND: THE LIFE OF RACING LEGEND JACK ZINK

Skills Workshop" for women aged fourteen and older on October 2, 2004. Dedicated to providing interactive educational outdoor opportunities for women, the workshop offered classes in muzzle loading, Dutch oven cooking, feather craft, fly fishing, basic auto mechanics, and self defense.

Reflecting some of Jack's favorite pastimes, the Zink Ranch hosted a long list of racing events, which started with motorcycles in the 1960s and grew into both road races and off-road races in the 1970s. In the early 1990s, after hosting a number of two-day enduro races, Jack asked his friends with the Tulsa Trail Riders Association what their "big event" would be if they had the opportunity to host it. They said it would be the International Six Day Enduro, which alternated between the United States, Europe, and South America. Jack, always looking for the best competition, said that should be their goal.

In 1994 the Association put in a bid for the event and won. They put together a team for tactical and logistical support and started preparing the Ranch for five events a day, six days in a row. They laid out 300 miles of trails, using different combinations each day to create about 150 to 170 miles of intense riding. The top ten riders, in order of their finish, came from Italy, Sweden, Czechoslovakia, Germany, Finland, Australia, Portugal, Canada, the United States, and the Netherlands. According to several veterans with the "Six Day," the Zink Ranch enduro was the best they had ever seen.

For Jack, hearing such high praise for the Ranch became increasingly satisfying. By 2004 the Zink Ranch meant more to him than just a home or a retreat from the city and the world of business. It had become more than land and water and woods, more than a place to build roads and buildings and lakes. While he was justifiably proud of his business accomplishments and his racing exploits, nothing held a place in his heart like the Ranch. For Jack, the Zink Ranch was a place where people could get close to nature, test themselves, and rediscover the joy of being with friends, doing something they loved, and learning something about the world around them. For Jack, the Zink Ranch was his gift to the future.

When Jack told his wife, Jan, they were going to the Mediterranean to sail, she thought it would be on an ocean liner. Instead, Jack took the wheel and sailed them from island to island.

Jack, seen here with his friend, Henry Bellmon, was inducted into the Oklahoma Hall of Fame in 1989. Coming as no surprise to his friends and family, the theme for his acceptance speech was "honor."

Bobby Unser, the veteran racecar driver who had known Jack for several decades, traveled to Oklahoma City to honor his friend at the Oklahoma Hall of Fame induction ceremony. At the microphone in front of a statewide audience watching the ceremony on television, Unser tried to capture the spirit of the man being honored. "Jack," he said, "has always had a sense of urgency to make things happen. He has a fierce pride in his native Oklahoma. And he has always been an innovator." Unser listed the many accomplishments along the road, such as the awards received, the patents earned, the services rendered, the races won, but he finished by listing Jack's four commandments: Associate with successful people, understand who you are, be a dreamer, and have patience.

Jack responded with typical humility and grace. "On my honor...," he began, followed with a pause, "those are the first words of the Boy Scout oath...honor is the one ingredient that moves individuals, cities, states, and nations to greatness...it is the very fiber of fairness that all outstanding scouts, soldiers, business people, statesmen, volunteers, and competitors have in common." He looked around the room, thanked his many friends for attending, and marveled at the fact that he was joining a list of Oklahomans who had made the state such a great place to live. "I would like to leave you with a short rhyme that has meant a lot to me," he said:

"A winner is an average man,
*   Not built on any particular plan,*
Not placed with any particular luck,
*   But steady and earnest and full of pluck.*
A winner is a man who works,
*   Neither labor nor trouble shirks,*
He uses his hands, his head, his eyes,
*   The man who wins is the man who tries."*

For all of those in the crowd that night, and countless others whose paths he had crossed, Jack Zink was a true winner.

In 1989 Jack Zink was inducted into the Oklahoma Hall of Fame. It was neither the first award he had ever received, nor would it be the last, but in many ways it may have been the most significant. Most of the other awards were earned for excellence in one field of endeavor or another. Oklahoma State University inducted him into the Engineer's Hall of Fame for his innovations in industry and granted him the Henry G. Bennett Distinguished Service Award for his good deeds. The United States Automobile Club named him to their board of directors and chairman of the engine committee because of his innovations in car design. And the Indianapolis Speedway inducted him into the Motor Sports Hall of Fame, reserved for the very best of the world's racing fraternity. The Boy Scouts of America awarded him the esteemed Silver Beaver Award for service to youth. The Oklahoma Hall of Fame, on the other hand, recognized him for the cumulative value of his contributions to the people of Tulsa, Oklahoma, and the nation.

Afterword

By Darton Zink

My father, John Smith "Jack" Zink, passed away on February 5, 2005, just weeks after the first draft of this biography was completed. Six days later, on February 11 we held a memorial service joined by hundreds of friends and family members at the Donald W. Reynolds Center on the campus of the University of Tulsa.

At that memorial service, I had the honor of presenting a eulogy for my father. The author of this book, Dr. Bob Blackburn, thought it would serve here as an appropriate afterword to the story you have just read. I offer it as my tribute to my mentor, my friend, my father.

———

Over the past week, it has been both interesting and touching for me and for the rest of the family to learn how other people perceived our father, brother, uncle, and husband. We have heard a great many flattering adjectives attached to Dad's name, but I think the comment heard most often refers to the amazing number and diversity of experiences Dad squeezed into a single lifetime. I think it may have been Joe Cappy who said that Dad did enough for several lifetimes. Those of us who have had years to observe Jack Zink at close range know this better than anyone.

You know by now about the patents he earned for inventions which have led the combustion engineering industry. You have heard about the races he won, the businesses he built, the boards on which he served, and his dedicated efforts to build a better community and a better world. But I would like to take just a moment to share some facts about Dad that may not be so widely known.

For instance, few of you would know that his love of research and experimentation was not confined to the various combustion testing facilities he worked in over the years. In fact, he often brought his love of adventure and experimentation home to the kitchen. I can personally tell you that you have not lived until you have tasted Jack Zink's special huevos rancheros smothered in honey...or his Osage County steak, cooked with a 5,000 degree acetylene flame...or his fried peanut butter and jelly sandwiches. In the kitchen, I can assure you that Jack Zink was no one trick pony.

Any member of the family can tell you that Dad was passionate about one's responsibility to "leave a place better than you found it." I think he was constitutionally incapable of exiting a bathroom without first soaping, scrubbing, and polishing the sink. His standard practice was to stop and wash a rental car before returning it to the airport. Once, when Dad and I had rented motorcycles to run an event in Baja, Dad insisted that we find a place in San Jose de Cabo where we could wash our cycles before returning them to be loaded on the trailer. I received a special award that night for taking the best care of the equipment. Dad, however, did not get an award because of a little scrape on the fender which only came to light when he washed all that mud off his cycle.

Speaking of Baja and motorcycles, some of you know that Dad's last Baja motorcycle event was the year he turned 73. I want to be clear about the fact that Dad did not give up motorcycles because he was too old to race...he quit, he insisted, because at 73, "it just takes too long to heal."

All of us who were related to Dad benefited from his passionate approach to life. His wife, Jan, said the other evening that Dad's refusal to believe there was anything she could not do has blessed her life and transformed her from a shy and sedentary person to a bona fide daredevil with injuries to prove it. My Aunt Jill would credit Dad, I believe, with sharpening her considerable debating skills. She remarked just the other day that with his death, she lost her favorite "sparring" partner.

Growing up, Neel, Whitney, and I thought everyone knew how to swim, snow and water ski, ride motorcycles, race sailboats, and pitch a tent in a field and camp out in the dead of winter. Today, when any of us exceeds expectations or beats a competitor or endures through difficult circumstances, we know that we owe Dad a great debt for proving to us that we are tough. The loss of our Dad is made bearable by the ever present lessons of life he shared with us over so many years.

I would like to leave you today with a good piece of advice which comes straight from Jack Zink. For many years he has had taped to his closet wall the "Boy Scout Law." It says that, "A scout is trustworthy, loyal, helpful, friendly, courteous, kind, obedient, cheerful, thrifty, brave, clean, and reverent." Once I asked Dad why he had this taped to the wall and he said, "You know the old saying Dart, 'Out of sight, out of mind.' Well, I think these words are a pretty good recipe for a life, and I want to make sure they are never very far out of my sight."

ENDNOTES

CHAPTER 1

1   Joe David Brown, "Whooping Baron of the Prairie," *Tulsa Magazine* (*Tulsa World*), 1963, pp. 60-68.

2   Jane Feagin Cheairs, "Mrs. John Zink's Insurance Against Boredom Her Interests," *Tulsa World*, November 7, 1951, p. 20; Interview with Jill Zink Tarbell, December 16, 2003, Tulsa, Oklahoma.

3   Interview with Jill Zink Tarbell, December 16, 2003.

4   Danney Goble, *Tulsa: Biography of the American City* (Tulsa: Council Oak Books, 1997), pp. 33-49.

5   Jim Henderson, "Zink Bash is Something," *Tulsa World*, June 8, 1969, pp. 10-11.

6   Cheairs, *Tulsa World*, November 7, 1951, p. 20.

7   Swannie Zink, *Chapel in Penthouse* (Rogers, Arkansas: Avalon Press, 1947), p. 14.

8   Cheairs, *Tulsa World*, November 7, 1951, p. 20.

9   Interview with Jill Zink Tarbell, December 16, 2003.

10 *Ibid.*; Fifteenth Census of the United States, 1930, Enumeration District 72-154, p. 224.

11 Interview with Jack Zink, December 17, 2003, Tulsa, Oklahoma.

12 Interview with Jack Zink, April 23, 2003, Tulsa, Oklahoma; Interview with Jill Zink Tarbell, December 16, 2003.

13 Interview with Jack Zink, April 23, 2003.

14 Interview with Jill Zink Tarbell, December 16, 2003; Interview with Jack Zink, April 23, 2003.

15 Interview with Jack Zink, September 11, 2003, Tulsa, Oklahoma.

16 *The Tower* (Tulsa: Cascia Yearbook Committee, 1945), pp. 36-38.

17 *Ibid.*; Interview with Jack Zink, September 11, 2003.

18 *Ibid.*

19 *The Tower*, p. 38; *The Cascia* (Tulsa: Cascia Hall High School), September, 1945, p. 2.

20 Interview with Jack Zink, December 17, 2003.

21 Interview with Jack Zink, April 23, 2003.

22 "John Zink: One of Petroleum's Outstanding Exponents of American Free Enterprise," *The BUDA Oilfielder*, January-March issue, 1948, pp. 20-21.

23 Goble, pp. 67-108.

24 *Tulsa City Directory* (Tulsa: Polks Directory, 1930), p. 59.

25 Bob Foresman, "Amazing Tulsan Builds Amazing Floor Furnace," *Tulsa Tribune*, March 11, 1947; Interview with Jack Zink, April 23, 2003.

26 Goble, pp. 135-153.

27 Foresman.

28 *Ibid.*

29 Brown, "Whooping Baron of the Prairie," p. 67.

30 "John Zink," *The BUDA Oilfielder*.

31 Galen Kurth, "Jack of all Trades," *Open Wheel Magazine*, pp. 80-90.

32 Interview with Jack Zink, December 17, 2003.

33 Interview with Jack Zink, April 23, 2003.

34 *Ibid.*

35 *Ibid.*

36 *Ibid.*

CHAPTER 2

1   Interview with Jack Zink, September 11, 2003.

2   Ibid.; *The Redskin* (Stillwater: Oklahoma A&M Yearbook Committee, 1951).

3   Interview with Jack Zink, September 11, 2003.

4   *Oklahoma City Times*, September 25, 1908, p. 6.

5   Board of Directors Minutes, State Fair of Oklahoma, August 1, 1913.

6   *Daily Oklahoman*, August 10, 1913.

7   Clarence Douglas, *The History of Tulsa, Oklahoma* (Chicago: S.J. Clarke Publishing, 1921), pp. 638-641.

8   *Daily Oklahoman*, June 12, 1938, p. 3.

9   Don Stauffer, "Evolution of Midget Racing," *Motorsport Magazine*, www.Motorsport.Com.

10   *Daily Oklahoman*, December 28, 1938, p. 11.

11   Gordon Eliot White, *Kurtis-Kraft: Masterworks of Speed and Style* (MBI Publishing Company, 2001), pp. 10-16.

12   *Ibid.*, pp. 27-29.

13   *Ibid.*, pp. 36-50.

14   *Ibid.*, p. 43.

15   *Ibid.*, pp. 49-50.

16   *Daily Oklahoman*, May 11, 1948.

17   Interview with Jack Zink, October 29, 2002, Tulsa, Oklahoma; White, p. 56.

18   *Daily Oklahoman*, October 1, 1946, p. 18.

19   Interview with Jack Zink, October 29, 2002.

20   Laymond Crump, "Midgets Roll Again Tonight Bigger and Better than Ever," *Daily Oklahoman*, May 17, 1948.

21   Crump, "Midget Racers Open Season at Fairgrounds Oval Tonight," *Daily Oklahoman*, May 11, 1948.

22   *Ibid.*

23   *Daily Oklahoman*, May 23, 1948.

24   Interview with Jack Zink, October 29, 2002.

25   Interview with Jack Zink, December 17, 2003.

26   "Official Point Standings," Lavely Racing Promotions, October 5, 1948.

27   Telegram from John S. Zink to Jack Zink, April 11, 1949; White, p. 66.

28   Edward A. Spilman, "Car Owner With Vision," *Speed Age*, February: 1956, pp. 78-80; Wally Wallis, "Entry Sought by Zink, Reece," *Daily Oklahoman*, undated clipping in the Zink Scrapbook, 1951.

29   Letter to Jack Zink, February 2, 1951, Zink Scrapbook; Interviews with Jack Zink, December 22, 2004 and July 25, 2003, Tulsa, Oklahoma.

30   Charles E. Baukal, ed., *The John Zink Combustion Handbook* (Tulsa: John Zink Company, 2001), pp. 15-28, 352, 614.

31   Interview with Jack Zink, December 22, 2004.

32   *Ibid.*

33   *Oklahoma City Times*, June 27, 1951, p. 19.

34   Ed Almquist, "Flip-Proofing a Stock Car," undated clip, no publisher.

35   Spilman, p. 80.

36   "Jack Zink Captures Stock Car Feature," undated clip in Zink Scrapbook.

37   Wally Wallis, "Troubles Hit Ruby in Stock Car Races at Taft," undated clipping in the Zink Scrapbook.

38   *Oklahoma City Times*, June 27, 1951, p. 19.

39   Interview with Dennie Moore, December 22, 2004, Tulsa, Oklahoma.

40   Spilman, p. 79.

CHAPTER 3

1   Rick Popely, *Indianapolis 500 Chronicle* (Lincolnwood, Illinois: Publications International, 1998), pp. 8-11, 90-91.

2   *Ibid.*, pp. 80-81, 90-91.

3   Interview with Mrs. M.A. (Bea) Walker, April 20, 2004, Oklahoma City, Oklahoma; Interview with Bill Jones, May 22, 2004, Indianapolis, Indiana.

4   Interview with Bill Jones, May 22, 2004.

5   *Ibid.*; "Green Qualifies for '500' Race in Zink Special," May 20, 1950, clipping in the Zink Scrapbook

6   Popely, pp. 92-95; Interview with Bill Jones, May 22, 2004.

7   Website on Indianapolis 500.

8   Popely, pp. 96-95.

9   Interview with Bill Jones, May 22, 2004.

10 *Ibid.*

11 Gordon Elliot White, *Kurtis-Kraft: Masterworks of Speed and Style*, pp. 8-11.

12 *Ibid.*, pp. 99-100; Roger Devlin, "Dreams Rest on Heavy Foot," *Tulsa Tribune*, March 10, 1952.

13 Kurth, "Jack of All Trades," pp. 83-84; Spilman, "Car Owner with a Vision," p. 80.

14 Spilman, p. 80.

15 Kurth, p. 84; Interview with Bill Jones, May 22, 2004; Interview with Jack Zink, July 25, 2003.

16 Popely, pp. 104-107; "Bad Carburator, Pit Stop Hurt Sooners," *Tulsa World*, May 31, 1952.

17 *Ibid.*

18 Website on Indianapolis 500; Jack Kelley, "John Zink Special is Speedway Threat," *Tulsa World*, March, 1953.

19 *Ibid.*; *Tulsa World*, May 5, 1953.

20 *Ibid.*

21 Popely, pp. 108-113.

22 *Ibid.*; Ed Spilman, "Tulsa Shop Has Eye on Indianapolis 500," *Tulsa Tribune*, February 22, 1954.

23 *Ibid.*; Spilman, "Car Owner with a Vision, p. 80.

24 Sal Veder, "How Fast?" *Tulsa World*, May 30, 1954; "John Zink Special Ready for Indianapolis," *Tulsa World*, April 25, 1954.

25 Popely, pp. 114-119; Spilman, "Car Owner with a Vision," p. 81.

26 Gary Wayne, *The Watson Years: When Roadsters Ruled the Raceway* (Marshall, Indiana: Witness Productions, 2001), p. 33; Interview with A.J. Watson, May 22, 2004, Indianapolis, Indiana.

27 Wayne, pp. 33-34.

28 Popely, pp. 96-119; Interview with A.J. Watson, May 22, 2004.

29 Interview with John Zink, December 22, 2004

30 White, pp. 104-114.

31 Ed Spilman, "Tulsan Tackles Indy 500 with New Car, Same Team," *Tulsa Tribune*, March 7, 1955; "Zink Driver Says Planning, Not Daring Won 500 Race," *New York Herald Tribune*, June 21, 1955.

32 Frank Blunk, "Auto Race Pit Gang Flagged as Unsung Victory," Undated clipping, Zink Scrapbook.

33 Ed Spilman, "Zink Race Team Harvests Sweet Fruits of Victory," *Tulsa Tribune*, June 6, 1955.

34 *Tulsa World*, May 31, 1955; Interview with A.J. Watson, May 22, 2004; Popely, p. 125.

35 Ed Spilman, "Zink Car Had Fuel to Spare After Victory in 500," *Tulsa Tribune*, May 31, 1955, n.p.

36 *Ibid.*

37 Popely, p. 120.

38 *Ibid.*

39 Spilman, Tulsa Tribune, May 31, 1955.

40 Ibid.

41 Ibid.

42 Ibid.; Interview with A.J. Watson, May 22, 2004; Jack Kelley, Tulsa World, May 31, 1955.

43 Spilman, Tulsa Tribune, May 31, 1955.

CHAPTER 4

1   Ed Spilman, "Zink Race Team Harvests Sweet Fruits of Victory," *Tulsa Tribune*, June 6, 1955.

2   "Fuel Shortage Gave Zink Anxious Time," *Tulsa World*, May 31, 1955.

3   "Zink Driver Clinches AAA Title; Eyes Triple Crown," *Tulsa Tribune*, September 12, 1955.

4   Ed Spilman, "Car Owner With Vision," *Speed Age*, February, 1956, pp. 27-28.

5   *Ibid.*

6   Wayne, *The Watson Years*, p. 65.

7   George Moore, "A.J. Given Free Hand on Zink Car," *Tulsa World*, May 3, 1956; "New Lighter Zink Special, Designed by Watson, Has Gasoline Alley in a Dither," *Tulsa World*, May 13, 1956.

8   Interview with A.J. Watson, May 22, 2004.

9   Spilman, "Car Owner with Vision," p. 81; Kurth, "Jack of All Trades," *Open Wheel*, p. 86.

10 *Ibid.*

11 Wayne, *The Watson Years*, p. 123.

12 *Ibid.*

13 *Ibid.*, p. 124; "Flaherty Feels Jinx is Whipped," *Tulsa World*, February 6, 1956.

14 Interview with A.J. Watson, May 22, 2004.

15 Ed Spilman, "Zink's Skinny Screamer May Jolt Racing Trade," *Tulsa Tribune*, May 21, 1956.

16 Ed Spilman, "Zink Race Garage Calm Amid Track's Turmoil," *Tulsa Tribune*, May 26, 1956.

17 *Ibid.*

18 "Second Entry from Tulsa Forced Out," *Tulsa Tribune*, May 30, 1956.

19 Popely, p. 130.

20 "Second Entry from Tulsa Forced Out," *Tulsa Tribune*, May 30, 1956; Frank Blunk, "Victory at Indianapolis Is Old Story to Zink Car Pit Crew," *New York Times*, June 10, 1956.

21 Ibid.

22 "Broken Throttle Arm Almost Cost Zink Car '500' Victory," *Tulsa Tribune*, May 31, 1956.

23 *Ibid.*; R.K. Shell, "Winner Gulps Milk First, Then Kisses," *Indianapolis Times*, May 31, 1956.

24 "Zink Racing Team May Become New American Track Dynasty," *Tulsa World*, May 31, 1956.

25 *Ibid.*; "Official Finish, 1956 Indianapolis 500," document in the Zink Scrapbook.

26 Spilman, "Car Owner With Vision," p. 26; *Tulsa World*, March 29, 1954; Jack Kelley, "Zink Stock Car Wins Marathon Race Here," *Tulsa World*, May 30, 1955.

27 "Race Contract to John Zink," *Tulsa Tribune*, February 20, 1956; "Zink Awarded Local Stock Car Contract," *Tulsa World*, February 21, 1956.

28 "Zink Enters NASCAR Race," *Tulsa Tribune*, August 1, 1956.

29 Kurth, p. 89.

30 "Zinks Get New Racers," *Tulsa World*, November 30, 1956; "Zink Enters NASCAR Race," *Tulsa Tribune*, August 1, 1956; "Cancelled Race is Costly," *Tulsa Tribune*, August 6, 1956.

31 *Ibid.*

32 Kurth, p. 89.

33 "To Seek U.S. Stock Car Records," *National Speed Sport News*, December 17, 1957.

34 Ed Spilman, "Zink Team May Spring Surprise at Speedway," *Tulsa Tribune*, no date.

35 Wayne, *The Watson Years*, pp. 125-126.

36 Jack Kelley, "Zink Car Damaged," *Tulsa World*, May 29, 1957.

37 Ed Spilman, "Zink Racer a Victim of Extra Lap," *Tulsa Tribune*, May 30, 1957.

38 Wayne, *The Watson Years*, pp. 8-9.

39 Ed Spilman, "Zink Team is Invited to Italian Race 'Olympics'" *Tulsa Tribune*, November 26, 1956; "To Monza Victory in Zink Special," *Tulsa World*, June 29, 1958; Wayne, *The Watson Years*, p. 9.

40 George Moore, "Zink Setting Practice Pace at Speedway," *Tulsa World*, May 11, 1958; "Flaherty Fails 500 Physical," *Tulsa World*, May 6, 1958.

41 "Two Zink Cars Get First Row," *Tulsa World*, May 17, 1958.

42 Ed Spilman, "Great Driving by Reece Brightened Dismal 500," *Tulsa Tribune*, May 30, 1958; Popely, pp. 138-139.

43 *Ibid.*

44 *Ibid.*, p. 143.

45 *Ibid.*

46 Wayne, *The Watson Years*, pp. 129-130.

47 "To Monza Victory in Zink Special," *Tulsa World,* June 29, 1958.

48 Kurth, p. 87; Interview with Jack Zink, December 22, 2004.

49 Interview with A.J. Watson, May 22, 2004.

50 Wayne, *The Watson Years*, pp. 48-49.

51 *Ibid.*; Interview with A.J. Watson, May 22, 2004; Interview with Jack Zink, December 22, 2004.

52 Wayne, *The Watson Years*, p. 90.

53 "Zink Sending Two Tulsa Racers After Third Victory on Indianapolis Track," *Tulsa World*, May 29, 1959.

54 *Ibid.*

55 Tom Lobaugh, "Zink Car Takes Ninth Place in Classic: Flaherty Crashes," *Tulsa World*, May 31, 1959.

56 Ed Spilman, "Zink Team Undaunted by Indianapolis," *Tulsa Tribune*, June 1, 1959.

57 *Ibid.*

58 *Ibid.*

59 "Axle Woes Flag out Tulsa Entry," *Tulsa World*, May 31, 1960; Popley, p. 161; "Zink Court Holds Plush Camp Out," *Tulsa World*, May 29, 1961.

60 "Popularity of Turbines on Rise," *Tulsa World*, March 4, 1962.

61 Ed Spilman, "New Zink Car," *Tulsa Tribune*, July 24, 1961; Ed Spilman, "Zinks Cinderella Car Delays Race Debut," *Tulsa Tribune*, May 27, 1961.

62 "Zink Planning Turbine Engine," *Tulsa World*, May 26, 1960.

63 "Zink is Still Optimist Despite Big Reversal," *Tulsa Tribune*, May 1, 1962.

64 *Ibid.*

65 Kurth, p. 88; "Zink Released from Hospital After Accident," *Tulsa Tribune,* May 4, 1962.

66 *Ibid.*; "Zinks 500 Car May Get Bumped," *Tulsa World*, May 19, 1962.

CHAPTER 5

1   Jim Henderson, "A Zink Bash is Something," *Tulsa World*, June 8, 1969.

2   *Ibid.*; Untitled clipping, *Tulsa Tribune*, November 14, 1961.

3   Henderson, "A Zink Bash is Something," *Tulsa World*, June 8, 1969.

4   *Ibid.*

5   "Zink Tries to Sell All Over the World," *Tulsa World*, July 28, 1963.

6   "Tulsa Firm Plans to Make Cooling Units," *Tulsa World*, September 17, 1952; "Tulsa Burners Used to Make Rocket Fuels," *Tulsa Tribune*, May 25, 1961.

7   "Zink Tries to Sell All Over the World," *Tulsa World*, July 28, 1963; Interview with Jack Zink, December 22, 2004; "Zink to Build New Plant in London Area," *Tulsa Tribune*, November 7, 1963; "Zink Expands Here, Adds Foreign Plants," *Tulsa World*, January 10, 1965; "Zink Puts Stress on Foreign Trade," *Tulsa World*, April 12, 1964.

8   "Housewives in England Know Zink," *Tulsa World*, July 5, 1964; "Zink Expands Here, Adds Foreign Plants," *Tulsa World*, January 10, 1965; "Zink Foreign Growth Seen," *Tulsa World*, October 15, 1967.

9   "Zink Company Builds Extensive Lab Facility," *Tulsa World*, March 16, 1969.

10 "Zink in Commercial Cooling Market," *Tulsa Tribune*, May 11, 1970.

11 "Zink Product Fights Pollution," *Tulsa World*, September 12, 1965.

12 *Ibid.*

13 "Air Study Group Planned by Zink," *Tulsa World*, January 19, 1969.

14 Untitled clipping, *Tulsa World*, January 10, 1965; "Work Launched by Zink at New Skiatook Plant," *Tulsa World*, October 25, 1966.

15 "Zink Plans to Switch to Conventional Car," *Tulsa World*, March 24, 1963; "Zink Racer Stretches Name to Mouthful," *Tulsa World*, March 4, 1963.

16 "Zink Car Crashes," *Tulsa World*, May 12, 1963; "Zink Reports Trackburner Ready to Go," *Tulsa Tribune*, May 29, 1963.

17 "Zink Racer Too Damaged to Compete at Milwaukee," *Tulsa World*, June 1, 1963.

18 Interview with Bill Jones, May 22, 2004; Interview with Jack Zink, July 25, 2003.

19 "Pair of Jacks Good Race Hand," *Tulsa Tribune*, January 7, 1964.

20 "Zink Car Makes 500; Mechanic is Hurt," *Tulsa Tribune*, May 23, 1964; "Brawner Joins Zink Crew as Moore's Sub," *Tulsa World*, May 28, 1964.

21 "Zink Crew Wishes 'Old' Offy Had Been Used," *Tulsa World*, May 31, 1964; Interview with Dennie Moore, December 22, 2004.

22 Interview with Bill Jones, May 22, 2004; "Trackburner Gets New Name But Same Job-Beat Fords," *Tulsa Tribune*, April 22, 1965; Kurth, p. 88.

23 "Engine Trouble Puts Zink Racer Behind Schedule," *Tulsa World*, May 13, 1965; Polk, p. 185.

24 "Zink Race Car Second in Nation," *Tulsa Tribune*, December 22, 1965; Interview with Bill Jones, May 22, 2004; "Ford Powers New Zink Car," *Tulsa Tribune*, December 29, 1965; "New Zink Racer to be Unveiled," *Tulsa World*, March 20, 1965; "City Firm Given Task of Curing Racing Woes," *Tulsa World*, April 10, 1966.

25 "New Zink Trackburner Wins in First Outing," *Tulsa Tribune*, March 21, 1966.

26 "Zink Mulls Protest in Third Place Finish," *Tulsa World*, May 31, 1966.

27 "Pit Stop Costly to Zink," *Tulsa Tribune*, May 31, 1966.

28 *Ibid.*; "Zink Special in New Bid for Points," *Tulsa Tribune*, September 8, 1966.

29 "McElreath Conquers Extra Stops," *Tulsa World*, June 1, 1967.

30 "Zink Has Knack for Sailing Too," *Tulsa Tribune*, July 10, 1964.

31 John Barnes and Mike Yates, "The Lightning in Skaneateles," International Lightning Class Website.

32 "Zink Has Knack for Sailing Too," *Tulsa Tribune*, July 10, 1964.

33 "Zink Captures Regatta Prize," *Tulsa World*, October 7, 1968; "Zink Tops Sailboat Field," *Tulsa Tribune*, June 23, 1967; "Tulsa's Zink Takes Trophy," *Tulsa World*, October 31, 1968; "Zink Tops Sailboat Field," *Tulsa Tribune*, June 23, 1967; "Zink Captures Lightning Class Sailing Race on Heels of Baja," *Tulsa World*, June 24, 1975.

34 "Cagle Car Obtains Moore of a Facelift," *Tulsa World*, March 24, 1969.

35 *Ibid.*

36 *"Hahn-Zink Racing Combine Finished; New Ride Unlikely,"* *Tulsa* World, March 15, 1981.

37 "Zink, Large Industrial Heater Firm, Will be Sold to Sunbeam," *Tulsa World*, December 4, 1969.

38 *Ibid.*

39 "Sunbeam to Acquire Zink Firm," Tulsa Tribune, February 26, 1972; "Jack Zink a Sunbeam Director," *Tulsa World*, June 22, 1972.

40 "Zink Plans Six Burner Courses," *Tulsa Tribune*, January 29, 1972; "John Zink Burner School Open," *Tulsa Tribune*, January 29, 1972; "42 Complete Burner Course," *Tulsa World*, July 23, 1975.

41 "Foreign Engineers Visit Zink," *Tulsa Tribune*, May 18, 1979.

42 U.S. Department of Commerce, Bureau of Economic Analysis.

43 "Zink Means Business in Pollution Control," *Tulsa Tribune*, May 7, 1970.

44 "Zink Forecasts Good Year for Tulsa Firm," *Tulsa Tribune*, June 29, 1979.

45 "Two Stage Burner to be Made Here," *Tulsa Tribune*, December 17, 1979; "Unburnable Oil Made Burnable," *Tulsa World*, August 19, 1981.

46 "Zinks Overseas Officers Take Cram Course," *Tulsa Tribune*, May 7, 190; "John Zink Singled Out," *Tulsa Business Chronicle*, May 16, 1983.

47 "Zink Told to Bargain," *Tulsa Tribune*, December 16, 1971; "Bargaining Order Directed at Zink," *Tulsa World*, May 12, 1972.

48 "Zink Estate Selling Sunbeam Corp Shares," *Tulsa World*, January 7, 1974; "Zink Disssents from Decision by Sunbeam," *Tulsa Tribune*, September 29, 1981; "Sunbeam Agrees to Takeover," *Tulsa World*, October 14, 1981; "Zink Completes Sunbeam Stock Sale," *Tulsa Tribune*, October 31, 1981.

CHAPTER 6

1   "Cycle Enduro Races Growing," *Tulsa World*, April 6, 1968.

2   "Adventurous Zink Finds Baja Rough," *Tulsa World*, November 6, 1972.

3   *Ibid*.

4   "Zink Getting Prepared for Outing in Baja," *Tulsa World*, May 27, 1973.

5   *Ibid*.

6   *Ibid*.; "Zink, Moore Third in Baja," *Tulsa World*, June 9, 1973.

7   "Baja Off-Road Race Steers Drivers into Danger," *Tulsa Tribune*, August 1, 1974.

8   "Zink Set for Baja 500 Run," *Tulsa World*, June 8, 1975; "Zink Charge Conquered Baja Course," *Tulsa World,* June 17, 1975.

9   *Ibid*.

10 *Ibid*.

11 "Leading Zink Car Halted by Mishap," *Tulsa World*, February 2, 1975.

12 "Zink Crashes; Escapes Injury," *Tulsa Tribune*, February 8, 1979.

13 "Zink Faces the Loss of More Than Races," *Tulsa Tribune*, June 6, 1976.

14 "Zink Plans Local Off-Road Race," *Tulsa World*, August 10, 1975; "Off Road Race Slated at Zink," *Tulsa World*, March 22, 1978.

15 "Zink Gets SORE Driving in ZORR," *Tulsa World*, February 6, 1977; "Zink Faces the Loss of More Than Races," *Tulsa Tribune*, June 6, 1978.

16 *Ibid*.; "Zink Charge Conquered Baja Course," *Tulsa World*, June 17, 1975.

17 "Chief of Tulsa Firm Eyes Race for Senate Seat," *Tulsa World*, March 10, 1979.

18 "Zink Resigns as Firm Head to Campaign," *Tulsa Tribune*, October 8, 1979.

19 "Zink Lambasts Stand on Cuba," *Tulsa World*, October 3, 1979; "Status of GOP Debate Remains Up in Air," *Tulsa World*, August 22, 1980.

20 "Zink's Alliance," editorial in the *Tulsa World*, October 16, 1979; "Zink Energy Alliance Proposal Gains Support," *Tulsa Tribune*, December 1, 1979.

21 "Energy at Issue for Hopefuls," *Tulsa World*, June 8, 1980.

22 "GOP Hopefuls Questioned by Foes of ERA," *Tulsa Tribune*, June 10, 1980; "Zink Bases Campaign on Business Experience," *Tulsa Tribune*, August 15, 1980.

23 *Ibid*.; "Provide Americans the Tools to Cure Inflation, Zink Says," *Tulsa Tribune*, March 9, 1979.

24 "Tulsa Businessmen to Aid Zink Campaign," *Tulsa Tribune*, November 5, 1979; "Tulsans Promise Zink Support," *Tulsa World*, May 15, 1980; "Senate Contenders List Contributions," *Tulsa Tribune*, May 9, 1980.

25 "Bette Zink Rides Campaign Trail on Horse Named George," *Tulsa Tribune*, April 25, 1980.

26 *Ibid*.

27 "Zink at Home on the Stump As Well as in the Shop," *Tulsa World*, August 17, 1980; "Zink-Kerr Out Front," *Tulsa Tribune*, August 13, 1980.

28 *Ibid*.; "GOP Hopefuls Dispute Who's Number 1," *Tulsa World*, July 25, 1980.

29 "Zink Radio Interview Gives Little Time to Religious Issues," *Tulsa Tribune*, September 8, 1980.

30 "Zink Stands Out," *Tulsa World*, August 22, 1980.

31 "Zink Hires Two in Staff Shake-Up," *Tulsa Tribune*, September 2, 1980.

32 "Zink Says No. 2 Blessing in Disguise," *Tulsa World*, August 27, 1980.

33 "Zink Blames Himself for Loss in Runoff," *Tulsa Tribune*, September 17, 1980; "Early Favorites Bow," *Tulsa World*, September 17, 1980.

34 Interview with Jack Zink, August 15, 2003, Tulsa, Oklahoma.

35 "Zink Asks TIA For Financing to Buy Tract," *Tulsa Tribune*, October 30, 1981.

36 Vickie Hawkins, "The Three Faces of Jack Zink," *Tulsa World*, June 2, 1987; Interview with Darton Zink, August 15, 2003, Tulsa, Oklahoma.

37 Interview with Darton Zink, August 15, 2003.

38 *Ibid*.

39 *Ibid*.

40 Zeeco Websites.

41 Interview with Jack Zink, August 15, 2003.

42 "Zink to be Chairman of Hillcrest Benefit," *Tulsa Tribune*, July 6, 1982; Untitled article in *Tulsa World*, November 8, 1977.

43 "Fairgrounds Authority Adds Zink" *Tulsa World*, April 18, 1981; "Jack Zink Named Chairman of Authority on Fairgrounds," *Tulsa World*, January 19, 1982.

44 Gary Percefull, "Zink Might Be Fairest For Fair," *Tulsa World*, February 14, 1982.

45 *Ibid.*

46 *Ibid.*

47 *Ibid.*

48 *Ibid.*

49 Interview with King Kirchner, Tulsa, June 7, 2004.

50 *Ibid.*

51 Interview with David Morgan, Tulsa, June 7, 2004.

52 *Ibid.*

53 The Foundation Center Web Site; Form 990s for the John Steele Zink Foundation.

54 "City Approves Zink Lake Name," *Tulsa World*, August 28, 1982; "Aquafest to Celebrate Dedication of Zink Lake," *Tulsa World*, September 2, 1983.

INDEX